Here's what they're saying about Ed Hearn and his book, Conquering Life's Curves.

"Ed Hearn has taken life's curves and turned them into a grand slam!"
James F. Hennig, President, The National Speakers Association

"Ed has my deepest respect. Few men have faced life's challenges with such courage and grace. We can all learn greatly from him. He has a genuine desire to lift others to the top of life's mountain."
Fred Wilpon, Co-Owner, New York Mets

"Ed Hearn's story is truly inspirational. Ed's character and faith pulled him through seemingly insurmountable challenges. He is definitely a champion in the game of life."
Mario Mandina, President, National Lawyers Association

"As a major league catcher, Ed Hearn learned to deal with anything thrown at him. Ed's inspirational story isn't so much about the life's challenges that were thrown his way, but about how a champion responds to those challenges."
Brad Plumb, President, The North American Speakers Bureau

"Ed Hearn is truly an inspiration to all. He gives each of us a new outlook on life and what it takes to reach those goals which seem so impossible to achieve."
Karen Woods, MCI Consumer Markets Communications Manager

"Ed Hearn is a big man, with a big heart! His caring heart for people certainly stems from a loving heart for God. His courage to make himself vulnerable and share his trials results in a very powerful message."
Harry Lloyd, Founder and Chairman, House of Lloyd

"So many times we get caught up in our day-to-day activities, but Ed's message sheds a wonderful light on the truly important aspects of daily life."
James G. Perilstein, First Vice President, Merrill Lynch

"Ed Hearn speaks from the heart and carries a powerful message. He is a champion in every way—whether on the field or off."
David J. Fiser, Vice President, Kansas Farm Bureau Insurance

"Ed conquers life's curves by hitting a home run off *The Inside Pitch*. The Lord has given him the strength and will to have true success and a real impact for eternity."
Dal Shealy, President/CEO, National Fellowship of Christian Athletes

"Blessed is the man who perseveres under trials, because he has stood the test, he will receive the crown of life God has promised to those who love him. Ed Hearn is God's man."
John Erickson, Assistant Commissioner, Big Eight Conference

"What Ed Hearn has endured is amazing. Only a man of Ed's character and faith could have survived the challenges he has faced. A winner by any measuring stick."
Ray Wilkins, Vice President, Southwestern Bell Telephone

"The true heart and soul of a man is exposed in the face of dark times. Ed Hearn has a heart and soul that shines like a guiding beacon in the night."
Bobby Bell, NFL Hall of Fame Linebacker, Kansas City Chiefs

"Ed's humorous reflection on his own life's experience, coupled with his sensitive treatment of life's challenges, is an electrifying combination."
Jeff Wilson, Sprint, Director of Advanced Learning Strategies

———

"After reading *Conquering Life's Curves*, you may not remember Ed Hearn so much as a ball player, but more as a man who will have genuinely touched your life."
Herk Robinson, Exec. VP/General Manager, Kansas City Royals

"Ed is an awesome living example of how, with a persevering attitude, we can overcome even the biggest obstacles in our lives."
Nancy Lauterbach, President, Five Star Speakers Bureau

"Ed's story is one of courage, inspiration and motivation. His climb to the big leagues prepared him for the 'Biggest Game' involving all of us. . .life. Ed Hearn is not only a winner but someone who serves as a role model by being one of life's champions."
Steve Palermo, Special Assistant to the M.L.B. Executive Council

"We are told in Scripture that if we love the Lord, whatever happens will turn out for the good. Ed Hearn's life is a great example of this truth. His message is one we all need to hear."
Bobby Bowden, Head Football Coach, Florida State University

"*Conquering Life's Curves* is inspirational, provocative, witty, sad, wise and wonderful."
J.C. Watts, U.S. Congressman, R-Oklahoma

"I have known Ed for a long time, and I know you will be amazed at what he has gone through during the last ten years. His story is a true testimony of the love of Jesus Christ in a person's life, because only by the strength of God could a human being endure what Ed went through."
Kevin Seitzer, Milwaukee Brewers, Third Baseman

CONQUERING LIFE'S CURVES

Baseball, Battles
& Beyond

with Gene Frenette

A Division of Howards W. Sams & Company

Published by Masters Press
A Division of Howard W. Sams & Company
2647 Waterfront Pkwy. E. Dr. Suite 100, Indianapolis, IN 46214

© 1996 by Ed Hearn
All rights reserved. Published 1996
First Masters Press Edition November 1996

Printed in the United States of America

ISBN 1-57028-130-0

96 97 98 99 00   10 9 8 7 6 5 4 3 2 1

Library of Congress Cataloging-in-Publication Data Pending

Unless otherwise indicated, all Scripture quotations are from the *Holy Bible, New International Version,* © 1973, 1978, 1984, International Bible Society. Used by permission of Zondervan Bible Publishers. Other quotations are taken from *New American Standard Bible,* (NASB) © The Lockman Foundation 1960, 1962, 1963, 1968, 1971, 1972, 1973, 1975, 1977, the *Revised Standard Version of the Bible* (RSV) © 1946, 1952, 1971, 1973, the *Authorized/King James Version* (KJV).

Cover illustrator: Jeff Sharpton
Phil Velikan

Dedication

This book is dedicated to the two most precious people in the world to me—my beautiful wife, Tricia, and my seventeen-month-old son, Cody.

To Tricia, because I can honestly say that without you by my side for the past eight years, I would not be here to write these words. Your love, inspiration and dedication have meant more to me than words could ever express.

To Cody, because I want you, my son, to one day be able to look back on my days before you came along. I have so much love to share with you. I hope that I am blessed with the health to be there for you, as my father was for me.

———

Family Time

We would like to give a special thanks to our families for all their encouragement. Without them, neither of us would have been in a position to write this book.

To my parents, Bill and Jeanne Hearn, who were willing to sacrifice so much in order to dedicate their lives to raising a strong, close-knit family.

To my brother and sister, Tom Hearn and Debbie Shannon, for sticking with me through all the ups and downs.

To my grandmother, Mildred Tozour, for being the best granny a guy could ever have.

To my late grandparents, Jack Tozour and Ted and Myra Hearn, whose memory I hold dear to my heart.

To my wife Tricia's parents, Heinz and Ursula Trienens, for raising a very special daughter.

To my brother-in-law, Thomas Trienens, for his ongoing support and friendship.

Ed

I'd like to thank my wife, Dot, and the three children we love so much—Sean, Joseph and Kelly—for their unfailing support of me co-authoring this book. Without Dot's encouragement, especially around the holidays when I was either writing at the University of North Florida or in Kansas City, this book could never have been completed on time. It definitely helps to be married to the world's greatest wife when you're writing a book. I love you, honey.

To my parents, Roland and Yvette Frenette of Winooski, Vermont, my sincere appreciation for all their love, support and loyalty over the years. May God bless you and keep you.

Gene

———

Contents

Foreword

To Ed Hearn, *Conquering Life's Curves* is more than just the title of a book. He has courageously battled "curves" that would make hitting off Nolan Ryan seem like a breeze. I know. I have seen the impact of both.

A February 27, 1995, *Sports Illustrated* cover story about the misadventures of "Dead End Kids" Dwight Gooden and Darryl Strawberry described the 1986 Mets as "a portable party driven by alcohol, amphetamines, gambling, and drugs." Clean-living catcher Gary Carter was depicted as being part of the team's "underwhelming minority," a group that also included Hearn, Carter's backup behind the plate.

What has happened to Dwight, Darryl and Ed since those days is a perfect example of why people should never judge a player completely by his on-the-field performance. As syndicated columnist Erma Bombeck once wrote: "Do not confuse fame with success. Madonna is one. Helen Keller is the other."

Gooden and Strawberry certainly went on to more fame than Hearn in baseball, but after seeing the road each has traveled, there's no question in my mind which one found the true meaning of success. Ed has taken some of the worst knockdown pitches the game and life have to offer, and has persevered.

Anyone who has faced great challenges of any kind will find his story uplifting. It's as inspirational as anything I've ever encountered in or out of baseball.

What makes Ed's story so compelling is that he had to deal with losing a baseball career, then nearly his life. Even now, he must take loads of medication so his body can perform normal functions that you and I take for granted. The real miracle here is that Ed is using his own adversity in a positive manner, to send a message in his public speaking that inspires audiences all around the country.

In 1986, Ed's rookie season, he was enjoying what players cherish above all else—being part of a World Series championship team. He certainly wasn't the star of the New York Mets, but scouts for the Kansas City Royals obviously liked what they saw. The following spring they traded a promising, home-grown, minor league pitcher named David Cone to get Hearn from the Mets. John Schuerholz, then our general manager, described our new backstop by saying, "This guy is solid in every way and could be our catcher for the next ten years."

We were excited. Ed seemed to be one of the final pieces to the puzzle in our quest to return to the great teams we had in the late seventies and early eighties. That was important because I wanted nothing more than to win another World Series before I retired.

But while David Cone would become a twenty-game winner in New York and twice lead the National League in strikeouts, Ed's career and his life changed dramatically. Pain in his throwing shoulder wouldn't go away in the early stages of the 1987 season. He underwent total reconstructive surgery, and for the next three years, he waged a courageous, but futile, battle to resurrect his once promising career. In the spring of 1991, Ed resigned himself to the sad truth that he would never play baseball again.

"The worst trade in Royals' history," said Ewing Kauffman, our late team owner.

Players come and go, but often the most difficult transition is the one into the real world. Some don't adjust well to life outside the batter's box.

I wasn't sure for a while how it would go for Ed. In May, 1992, I looked up into the stands at Kauffman Stadium just before the start of batting practice and barely recognized a man who a year earlier had been a strong, healthy professional athlete. Ed had just been released from the hospital after receiving a kidney transplant. Although he wasn't supposed to be around crowds of people, he had asked a friend of his, Rick Austin, to bring him out to the ball park. He just wanted so badly to hang out with the guys.

It was somewhat uncomfortable speaking with Ed as he sat slouched in the first row of the stands, barely able to speak complete sentences without stopping to catch his breath. It wasn't as if I had never stopped to share an encouraging word with someone who was sick or physically challenged. But this was different. This guy was one of us.

As batting practice started and I said good-bye, I walked away wondering why these kinds of things have to happen. I was reminded about how fortunate those of us on the field that day really were.

When I see this man in action today as a professional speaker, many of my concerns of that afternoon have been eliminated. Ed can't hit a baseball the way he used to, but he's bringing crowds to their feet by motivating people with an inspiring message. That's a special achievement for a man who at one time seemed to have lost everything.

When kids play baseball in the backyard these days, some might still pretend to be Dwight Gooden or Darryl Strawberry. They don't pretend to be Ed Hearn. But when adversity hit, it was Ed's courage and tenacity that makes him the one worthy of imitation.

In July, 1986, late-night talk show host David Letterman poked fun at all the Mets who had authored books. On national television, he then held up a phony hardback entitled, *Ed! The Ed Hearn Story*, a detailed account of each of Ed's 12 big-league hits. That drew laughs from coast to coast. But isn't it ironic that of all those literary efforts by some of baseball's biggest names, none will provide a message as enduring as the one told by a retired, second-string catcher with a bad arm?

Conquering Life's Curves is no fiction. It's a hard-hitting tale of Ed's struggles in and out of the game. It'll make you laugh and it'll make you cry. This is a story about the best kind of comeback. Ed has come full circle from a man who almost lost his life to a man who now empowers lives.

Injuries prevented Ed Hearn from ever proving himself with the Kansas City Royals, but he's proven himself in the game of life. His story is one of a true champion.

George Brett

Introduction

On June 4, 1994, I had the opportunity to speak at the College World Series breakfast in Omaha, Nebraska. After the breakfast was over and I had completed my presentation to the players, coaches and family members, I was busy greeting folks who wanted to pass on their appreciation for the message I had given.

Eventually, I was approached by a man who asked me if I had written any books about my life experiences. When I told him no, he responded in disbelief and strongly recommended that with my story, I should definitely write one.

I all but laughed in his face. But as I've seen the impact that my story has had on audiences and the requests I get for follow-up material such as a book or tapes, my attitude has changed. It has become very evident to me that, with all the challenges we face in our society, people want and need to hear words of encouragement and inspiration. Since our country seems to hold professional athletes in such high esteem, we have a tremendous opportunity to positively impact the lives of many people.

As you read this book, I would like you to put aside any preconceived notions that you may have of professional athletes. This book is much more than just another old jock's autobiography. If that was all I had to offer, I would not have taken the time and effort to write this book.

Certainly, I want you to enjoy my stories about the times I had as an athlete. But, more importantly, I hope you'll be able to find insight and encouragement from the tremendous peaks and valleys that I've experienced in the last decade.

The purpose of this book isn't just to relate tales about my baseball life in the minors, my season with the 1986 World Series champion New York Mets or my injury-filled time with the Kansas City Royals. I want to challenge and inspire you with stories of courage, faith and motivation. Not just my stories, but others' as well.

I believe the most valuable parts of this book are contained in little sections called "The Inside Pitch" at the end of each chapter.

These sections are a mixture of both opinion and anecdotes, which I hope provoke thought that positively impacts your life.

A lot of people have encouraged me in my struggle to overcome the challenges of the past few years. It's been a humbling experience to reach the point of joy and peace I know today. I hope this book, in some way, can do the same for you.

Putting this book together wouldn't have been possible without the assistance of many special people. I'm deeply indebted to the health professionals at St. Luke's Hospital in Kansas City who made my comeback possible: nephrologist Dr. Jim Mertz, my primary physician and his associates, Drs. Crouch, Woods and Sharma; Dr. Tom Helling and Dr. Paul Nelson, my transplant surgeons; immunologist Dr. Nabih Abdou, who treats my gamma globulin deficiency; pulmonologist Dr. Ann Romaker, who treats my sleep disorder; transplant coordinators Brenda Brewer and Linda Harte; home dialysis nurse clinicians Sandy Nelson and Connie Kleinbeck; and transplant clinic secretary Shirley Johnson.

I'd also like to express my appreciation to the entire New York Life Insurance team, especially Mike Reeves, Chris Delahoussaye, Troy Braswell and Rick Austin. My thanks to speakers' bureau executives Brad Plumb (North American Speakers Bureau) and Nancy Lauterbach (Five Star Speakers Bureau); Jay Horwitz, public relations director for the New York Mets; and Denny Trease, communications director for the Kansas City Royals.

A thank-you also to the Communications and Visual Arts Department at the University of North Florida, particularly Dr. Robert Bohle and Donna Oxford; Joe DeSalvo, executive sports editor of the Florida Times-Union; and special thanks to my co-author and friend, Gene Frenette. Without all his hard work, dedication and expertise, this book might never have materialized.

Most importantly, I'd like to thank my Creator, Savior and Lord Jesus Christ for all the many wonderful blessings He has given me; for the many challenges which have helped me to grow as a person; and for the strength and courage to overcome and learn from each of these difficult times. For without all this, there would be no book, story, or message to share with others.

1

From the Penthouse
to the Outhouse and Back

*O*n April 18, 1987, my phone rang at the Grand Hyatt Hotel in New York. It was Steve Schryver, the New York Mets' minor league director, telling me to meet him in the lobby. He didn't have to say what it was about.

I knew. I couldn't get down there fast enough.

Just three weeks earlier, the Mets had traded me to the Kansas City Royals for a minor-league pitcher named David Cone. I was back in town for a three-game series with the New York Yankees. Schryver, who brought me to the Mets in 1983, had something I couldn't wait to get my hands on.

The minute we sat down, he took out a small velvet box. Inside was something I never dreamed of owning: a World Series ring. Even now, almost ten years later, it gives me chills to think about it.

So many guys with Hall of Fame credentials—players like Dale Murphy, Ryne Sandberg, Don Mattingly—never experienced the joy of even being in a World Series. And here I was, after eight long years in the minors and one season in the big leagues, being given my own ring.

After Schryver left, I remember taking a walk with Tricia, my girlfriend at the time, down the street to have lunch. I don't think my feet even touched the ground.

On that day, at that moment, life was perfect. Absolutely perfect.

I'm strolling around New York City. I've got the ring. I've got the girl. And I've got a lucrative baseball future in front of me as the Royals' starting catcher.

My salary might have been only $85,000 that season, but in another three years—when the average salary for a five-year player would jump to $1.3 million—I'd have it all. I was pointed right in the direction of Easy Street.

That was a decade ago. Since then, I feel like I've lived three or four lives. Almost all of them in a valley so deep, I wondered if I'd ever make it back up the mountain.

It's amazing the curves life throws at you. All I was concerned about that day in New York was finding a safe place to keep my priceless World Series ring. I figured about now I'd just be coming to the end of my baseball career. Instead, I'm taking 34 pills a day just to stay alive.

The Bible tells us how God has a plan for each of our lives. The last few years, I've had a difficult time getting a handle on what His plan was for me. It kept switching all the time. And it never seemed to change in my favor.

In no time at all, I went from a promising major league catcher to someone many call the worst trade in Kansas City Royals history. The day after I got my World Series ring was really the beginning of the end of my baseball career.

I went one-for-four with an RBI against the Yankees and also had a monster collision at home plate with Dave Winfield, who bowled me over to score a run in the third inning. Winfield crashing into me wasn't the problem. It was my arm, which had been sore for a few weeks.

So after the game, the Royals decided it might be best for me to be put on the fourteen-day disabled list. Give my arm a little rest. Just a precautionary measure. No big deal, I thought.

Well, fourteen days on the DL turned into four weeks, then eight weeks, then a whole season. I had rotator cuff surgery and it would be sixteen months before I ever played again.

Those seven games with Kansas City at the end of the 1988 season would be my last in the big leagues. I spent the next two years trying to get back to the majors, but it finally became clear that nobody wanted a thirty-year-old catcher with a suspect arm.

OK, change of plans. Baseball and the potential to make millions of dollars are gone. What now? Where do I go from here?

I preferred a job where I could work with people. Finally, I settled on the insurance business with New York Life. It looked like a good opportunity. With my name recognition in the Kansas City area, I already had a built-in advantage to get into the door with some clients.

Hey, it wasn't as glamorous as playing Major League Baseball, but I had to start somewhere. Unfortunately, that start only lasted about five weeks before my life became one endless series of medical problems after another.

Kidney failure. An immune system deficiency. Dialysis. Sleep apnea. Kidney transplant. Bad reactions to prescription drugs. Loss of energy. Learning to sleep with a mask on my face. Constant diarrhea. A seventy-pound weight gain. Swallowing pill after pill. Depression.

If you're keeping score, that's about three years of pure hell.

Funny how we often think the grass is greener on the other side. If I only made as much money as someone else in the company, I'd really feel secure. If I only had a boat as big as my neighbor's, fishing would be a lot more fun. If I only had gotten that job transfer to another city, I'd be a lot happier.

I did the same thing at the 1986 World Series. In the bottom of the tenth inning of Game 6, I was thinking how nice it would be if I was in the other dugout. The Boston Red Sox were one out away from winning the Series and I thought, "Boy, I sure wish I was them, getting ready to swarm the field in celebration."

We always think somebody else has it better; that we have the worst end of the deal.

Maybe your coworkers make a lot more money, but they might have a lot more stress and other hidden problems that go along with their jobs. The neighbor's boat may be bigger. It may also break down more and force him to make costly repairs. Had you gotten the job transfer, maybe your spouse and children would have been miserable in their new surroundings.

God has a funny way of working things out sometimes. I'm sure glad now I wasn't in that Red Sox dugout. What a tough loss that would have been to live with. The tricky part for all of us is finding the good in what seems to be a negative situation. Taking the hand that's dealt us and turning it into something positive.

Growing up in south Florida, I was raised to believe that a person would never truly be happy until he did something for somebody else. I didn't fully understand what that really meant until I was forced to battle back from my own health problems.

Before I got sick, I thought a successful baseball career would be my opportunity to help others. I envisioned using my status as a major league ballplayer as a means of doing some good in the community.

When my career went down the tubes, I figured I'd be just another player who got hurt and went on with life. Then came a lot of suffering, which led me at one time to question whether it was worth even going on with life.

Again, I found myself wishing to be somebody else. Just anybody who didn't have to be in and out of the hospital, always stuffing pills into his mouth as if they were a bagful of peanuts.

It took a long time for God's plan to come into focus. I never realized until the last two years that so much good could come out of so much misery.

I went from a strong, healthy major league catcher to someone whose life became dependent on a machine and an organ from a stranger's body. Now I'm a motivational public speaker with a whole new platform.

No matter what, I wouldn't trade my life for anything. I know it's all been for a purpose.

I've still got the World Series ring. I married the girl. I see now that it's pointless to be concerned with what somebody else might have.

Life dealt me these cards. I'm playing them and it's exciting to see how the game is turning out.

The Inside Pitch

Inspiration

"Today's seeds are tomorrow's harvest."

Driving through my home state of Florida, you see row after row of trees filled with delicious oranges. If you're like me, your taste buds begin to water. It's time to reap the rewards from another miracle of the harvest.

Did you ever stop to think that every orange tree started with a tiny seed? Each has the explosive possibility of producing a healthy, strong tree filled each year with many bushels of oranges. Think how many thousands of times its weight that one little seed produces. The seeds you sow today will set in motion the harvest you will live with tomorrow.

Everything worthwhile starts as a tiny seed. Universally, this is known as the law of the harvest—you reap what you sow. Every day of your life, you are planting either good seeds or bad seeds. This applies not only to your own life, but also to the lives of others.

Yes, one seed of inspiration has the capacity to lift everybody. To spark the flicker of a smile on the face of a discouraged child. To raise the spirits of someone feeling overwhelmed by the daily grind. To actually change the course of another human being's day, week, year, or even lifetime.

I know. I am one of those seeds.

As you will see in the following chapters, my dreams were, at one time, quickly fading into ashes. But one day, in the fall of 1993, one man said something to me that would eventually help draw me out of the depths of my own depression. Without having any idea of the eventual impact his words would have on me, he planted a seed of hope which down the road led not only to the beginning of my speaking career, but also to the writing of this book.

To Brad Plumb, of the North American Speakers Bureau, I

will always be grateful. For it was his words at a business luncheon that changed my life. They inspired, encouraged, and uplifted my eyes to the wonderful opportunity I now have as I travel around the country, hopefully leaving my own trail of encouragement and inspiration.

My friend, Zig Ziglar, one of the greatest motivational speakers of all time, puts it this way: "The greatest good we can do for others is not just share our riches with them, but reveal theirs to them."

Now, if you contrast Brad Plumb with a bitter minor league manager that I played for late in my career, you will begin to understand that we can leave a trail of positive or negative seeds. This manager carried a big chip on his shoulder because he had never made it to the big leagues. Because of this, he left trails of cynicism and pessimism that often were destructive to the players he managed.

Whether we realize it or not, we all leave a trail of encouragement or destruction. This influence has an impact long after we are gone.

On a calm, crisp winter day, the cloudless blue sky will accentuate the long white vapor trail from a jet airline long after the plane is gone from sight. Like the airplane, all of us leave our own trail through life which can either inspire or hinder those around us.

Every person has the power to make others happy. As the old one-liner goes, some do it by entering the room, others by leaving the room. Which category applies to you?

Some people leave trails of hate and bitterness. Others leave trails of love and harmony. Some leave trails of selfishness and unconcern. Others leave trails of generosity and thoughtfulness.

What kind of seeds are you planting along the trail of your life? Think about it. It does make a big difference. Maybe an even greater difference than you could ever imagine.

2

Home Plate—
Where the Roots Run Deep

*Y*ou hear so much talk these days about how America isn't as strong as it used to be, partly because family units keep breaking down. So many kids are growing up in single-parent homes, shuffling back and forth from day care. It's all they can do sometimes just to get through a day. Many don't grow up in the kind of stable environment needed for them to develop a strong sense of discipline and self-esteem.

It wasn't until my pro baseball career had almost come and gone that I began to fully appreciate just how good I had it as a kid. I really had four parents because my Mom's folks, Jack and Millie Tozour, were as involved in our lives as anybody.

In my hometown of Fort Pierce, Florida, my favorite place of all was Granny and Grandpop's house. It was just a couple of miles up the road from the house I grew up in off the main highway, US 1. They moved from New Jersey to Florida when Grandpop's bursitis became so severe in his shoulders that he couldn't do carpentry work.

Grandpop bought thirteen acres of property on the north end of town, just south of Vero Beach, and a good chunk of it was marshland. He dug out the muck and topsoil, eventually starting his own dirt business after he retired from construction work. Out of that marshland, he created a beautiful, seven-acre pond that's as pretty as anything you'll see on a post card. It's home to all the geese, ducks and other waterfowl my Dad raises in his spare time. Eventually, our family and friends helped my parents build their dream house on that property in 1984. But during my childhood, going to "Lake Tozour" was as much my getaway as any baseball park, football field or fishing hole.

This place had it all—lots of space, Granny's cooking, Grandpop's character and the warm, secure feeling you got being

---

surrounded by nature. If a kid couldn't have fun there, something was wrong. It's where Dad often worked with me in developing my baseball skills, and where my younger brother, Tom, hit golf balls every day to become good enough to make it on the PGA Tour.

Just before nightfall, it's so peaceful there. The sunsets are awesome, and if you're looking for a good fight, grab a fishing pole. The bass in Lake Tozour are usually pretty accommodating.

You couldn't ask for a better environment to spend a childhood. Life at Granny's and Grandpop's, God rest his soul, was as good as it gets.

Ironically, I faced a lot of the same adversities in my early years that would test me as an adult. Sports, particularly baseball and football, was a big part of my life, but so were the medical problems that often baffled both my parents and doctors.

Just before my second birthday, I began having all kinds of physical ailments. I had everything from measles, to bronchial pneumonia, to strep infections, to persistent ear problems that required many surgeries. I bounced from doctor to doctor for years. Nobody could figure out the root of the problem.

I finally ended up at Shands Hospital in Gainesville. Doctors there basically told my Mom that she was a hypochondriac. One day, while I was being checked out, Mom read an article in the waiting room about all these problems that can set in when your immune system isn't normal. So she asked the doctors if I could have my immune system tested before we drove back to Fort Pierce.

The next day, doctors at Shands called back to report they had found the problem. It turns out the intuition of my hypochondriac Mom about her six-year-old son was right. The doctors said that the measles I had three years earlier damaged my gamma globulin and I couldn't properly fight off infection.

I eventually outgrew the problem, but not before taking these gamma globulin injections in the buttocks every four weeks for almost a year. I was fine after that. But little did I know that, twenty-five years later, my immune system would stop working again. Next time, the solution would be more complicated than just dropping my pants and being stuck by a needle.

Growing up, my parents were always around. They were poor as church mice when they got married, but they dumped their whole lives into us kids. My sister, Debbie, whom my parents adopted when I was three, brother Tom and I knew that Mom and Dad were right at our fingertips. They started their own printing business, which my Dad learned from his father, and built a shop right next to our house. They lived from paycheck to paycheck. We didn't have a lot in the way of extras.

My parents told us as early as junior high that there would be no funds for college, so we'd have to earn our way with scholarships of some kind. What they did give us was a foundation for how to be successful. All they asked in return was that we do our best in everything we did. Of course, Mom and Dad had no problem giving us a push. Looking back, I'm glad they did because I wasn't a tremendously disciplined kid, especially in high school.

It didn't matter to Mom and Dad what we chose to do, as long as we kept busy and out of trouble. We weren't allowed to watch too much television because they didn't believe in much idle time.

The number one rule was that whatever you did, you gave it one-hundred percent. Whether it was a Punt, Pass & Kick competition, Little League baseball game or peanut brittle sale for the YMCA (I sold $206 worth at age nine and won a bicycle), Mom and Dad made sure we gave it our all.

Almost from the time I was old enough to walk, there was no mistaking my love for sports. Football, baseball, basketball, golf. Whatever was in season, that's what I wanted to play. It's not as if I came out of the womb clawing for victory. The competitive aspect didn't really take hold until much later. Sports were just fun, which, for children, is supposed to be the whole point.

Dad and I spent so much time swinging the bat and playing catch in our backyard, I was pretty advanced by the time I started

T-ball at age six.

I hit my first home run for the Wildcats in the YMCA League, one of many teams that my Dad coached. The following year, I became interested in football and was given my first quarterback job in YMCA flag football by Pete Wells, who coached me at different points throughout my amateur career, including American Legion baseball.

But, as far as a mentor, nobody ever quite measured up to my Dad. He took an active role in helping me develop my skills. He did anything he could to help the other kids and me. He would read books on baseball strategy, watch videos, even go to coaching clinics to help us become better players. We used to drive two hours to Orlando every Saturday morning in the summer to attend clinics given by former major league catcher and manager Zack Taylor.

Dad was big on discipline. He'd put us through serious drills—rundown plays, game-situation hitting, exercise laps. He even put colored spots on the balls at batting practice to make us watch the ball better. In all my baseball years, even in the big leagues, I never had a better coach than Dad at teaching fundamentals. I'm not saying that would hold true for other major leaguers, but he knew best what worked for me.

Dad was the one who started me catching. I was eight-years-old playing B Little League ball for his Chandler Equipment team. Our catcher was picked up by an A team. My Dad knew the value of a good catcher in youth leagues and I think he just wanted to know if I was interested. So one day he brought home this big Army sack full of catching gear and dumped it on the floor. He asked if I wanted to try it on.

Catching had never crossed my mind until that night he brought the equipment home. I got down on the floor and put all the stuff on. It was something new, something cool. I went into the bathroom, found a long mirror so I could see everything. I was kind of like, "Wow! Yeah, let's give it a try."

The next couple of years, I started to realize that success meant not just playing for the fun of it, but also taking the game seriously. Our Turner Machine team dominated the Fort Pierce National Little League, going 25-0 one year. I did a lot of the catching, but also shared pitching duties with Roger Baird and Tommy Barber. It was about this time that Dad really started to instill in me the drive to succeed, but I have to tell you, it wasn't always fun the way he went about it.

Dad was really in his glory with that Little League team. He did a great job, especially molding kids who weren't that talented. Unfortunately, there were times it got to be very aggravating. Dad put up with a tremendous amount of jealousy from other teams' parents because we won so often. I didn't resent that as much as I did having to take Dad's criticism, especially when I least expected it.

I remember being in tears one night on the way home because Dad was getting on me about something that happened in the game. Then he said: "Look, Ed, if you don't want to do this, that's fine. You just tell me and I won't push you. But if you want to be good, this is what it's going to take." I said something like, "No, I want to do it Dad, really." But you know, at times, it was straining.

One game we played our main rivals, Tropigas. We were playing for the National League championship and they scored a couple of early runs off Roger Baird. My Dad came out of the dugout and I met him at the mound, expecting him to counsel Roger. Well, he got out there and didn't even give Roger a look. He looked right at me and chewed my butt out for calling the wrong pitches. My mouth dropped open. I turned to go back to catch and I was just furious. I was so mad, I had tears in my eyes.

The next inning, I came to bat and I just crushed a pitch for a home run. I had two home runs that day, plus a double in the bottom of the sixth that won the game, but I was still livid with Dad. He often brought that episode up to me during my professional career, suggesting that maybe I needed to get mad sometimes in order to perform my best.

It took me a long time to really appreciate what Dad did for me as a coach, in terms of understanding things he tried to do instead of resenting his criticism. To be honest, I was probably almost in the big leagues before I understood it all.

Even when Mom and Dad came out to watch me in the minors, I seemed to struggle, thinking Dad might start criticizing me like it was Little League all over again. But once I got to that level, he backed off quite a bit, basically giving me advice only when I asked. If I was in any kind of slump in pro ball, I never hesitated to get his opinion. More times than not, he was able to help me more just talking to me over the phone than some of my hitting instructors, simply because he knew the intricacies of my swing.

Dad was big on discipline and sacrifice, which often meant staying after games to work on something while other kids did their thing. Without Dad, I never would have made it half as far as I did in pro baseball. He instilled in me a work ethic that I needed to succeed.

Parents have to know just how much they can push. It's not always easy. Sports is a great way for kids to learn about success, working hard and paying the price. But there are extremes when it comes to parents pushing too much or simply not being involved at all. There's a fine line in the middle and I think I was pushed right to that line.

It was tough sometimes playing for my Dad. It was almost like playing for Vince Lombardi. You know, Lombardi's players didn't always like the way he coached. But in the end, they respected him and thanked him for the difference he made in their professional and personal lives.

One of my neatest baseball experiences came when Bruce Dixon and I were chosen to represent the Fort Pierce National Little League team as special guests of the Los Angeles Dodgers, who trained just a few miles north in Vero Beach. We got our pictures taken in the newspaper with Lee Lacey and a young infielder named Bill Buckner. Yes, the same Buckner who allowed the ball to skip under his glove at the 1986 World Series and my future teammate with the Kansas City Royals.

What made this day a little unusual for me was that I didn't grow up a Dodger fan. Not with Johnny Bench, my idol, playing for the Cincinnati Reds.

I never missed the Reds when they played the Dodgers at Holman Stadium. One day when I was about ten-years-old, I got brave, snuck behind the ropes and got a rosin bag that was on the Reds' warm-up mound. Later on, I remember the Reds loading the equipment into the busses. I was standing there, looking at Bench's mask sitting on top of an equipment bag with a number five on it. I was only a few feet away. I wanted to steal that thing so bad. Actually thought for a second about taking it, but I didn't.

In 1985, I finally met Bench in spring training. I never did get his autograph, but I bought one of his autographed jerseys from the 1970s. I'm mounting it on our wall for my son, Cody, along with Gary Carter's jersey and my own. A plaque under each will say: "Daddy's idol," "Daddy's mentor" and "Daddy's."

By the time I finished Little League, some decisions about my baseball future had to be made. The biggest one concerned school. I had been attending Saint Anastasia Catholic school from fourth grade through seventh grade. My parents had taken me out of public school because there was a lot of racial unrest at that time over desegregation. They didn't want me exposed to all the tension that caused.

In eighth grade, I transferred back to the public school system. Clyde Russell, the baseball coach at John Carroll, the Catholic high school, really hated to see me go. I actually tried to convince a couple other athletes to transfer with me, but I think they were afraid to go.

I just felt at the time that because Fort Pierce Central was a larger high school, I'd have more of an opportunity to become visible to major colleges and possibly to some professional scouts.

The other big decision concerned my position. Though I was becoming more comfortable as a catcher, most teams I played on definitely benefited from my pitching. I was an All Star pitcher. In the Little League championship game, we were up a run in the last inning and Dad was trying to save his pitchers. But the other team loaded the bases with nobody out, so he brought me in to pitch. I threw nine straight strikes and we won it.

But in working with Zack Taylor at his summer camps, he impressed upon me how different the throwing motion for pitchers and catchers really was. If I was serious about catching as my future, he said I needed to stick to that.

In the early 1970s, you heard a lot of talk at baseball camps about how catching was the easiest way to get to the big leagues because nobody wanted to do it. What was once a role of honor and responsibility had begun to be shunned by kids in favor of the more glorious positions such as pitcher or shortstop. I just can't understand why!

You don't want to play catcher? O.K., it does take a certain mentality to be a catcher.

If you don't believe that, just try it sometime. Suit up in armor like a warrior prepared for battle. Now squat for three hours and have Dwight Gooden throw ninety-five mile per hour fast-balls at you while a distracting bat is waved in your face.

Look out for those foul tips (the ones to the groin really feel great)! Count on broken fingers, bad knees and bruises the size and color of a ripe eggplant.

Meanwhile, you have to deal with all those temperamental personalities on the pitcher's mound. And, look out, here comes that two hundred pound runaway train barreling down on you trying to score from third! Now, quickly get up and rattle your bones back into place. On this next pitch, you have to throw the ball 127 feet, 3 and 3/8 inches on a dime within two seconds to second base.

"Great job, kid! Now get ready for the second game of the double-header!"

"Yes sir," I'd holler. I guess I was one of the few who had that crazed mentality. One thing about catching, though, really intrigued me. You were always part of the action. I was bored playing outfield, and even shortstop, in my young baseball days. Not catching. You always had to be on your toes.

By the time I got to Babe Ruth League at age thirteen, my pitching days were over. If I was going to make it in this game, there was only one place for me to be—behind the plate.

Though I idolized Johnny Bench, I never really thought of playing professional ball as an attainable goal until my Babe Ruth days. I began to look up to a catcher at Fort Pierce Central by the name of Donnie Yarborough, who was a seventh-round draft pick of the Minnesota Twins my freshman year of high school (1975).

My family was on vacation one time in the Appalachian Mountains and we went to see a couple rookie-league games in Elizabethton, Tennessee. That was a real thrill for me. I got to see Floyd Bannister, the number one draft pick and my future teammate with the Royals, pitch against Donnie's team.

That night, Floyd was throwing smoke and with the dim lights of this minor league field, hitters didn't have much of a chance. Since Donnie didn't play that game, I spent the night down in the bullpen talking to him as he was warming up pitchers during the game.

I thought that was really cool. Here was this hometown boy playing professional baseball.

Who knows? Maybe some day, that could be me.

The Inside Pitch

Family

*"There are two lasting gifts we can give our children—
one is roots, the other is wings."*

The term "family values" has become a big topic in recent years. Some people dismiss it as an overused cliché. I believe it can't be emphasized enough because without it, our country is headed for major trouble. We're already on a dangerous path because our priorities seem to be less geared toward strengthening families and more toward looking out for number one.

Since America was founded, we have been the envy of every country on this earth. Apart from our faith, no other entity can produce the positive impact on society that a close-knit family can. Not government. Not school systems. Not social programs. No matter how much money we as Americans pump into these things, it is all for naught if we do not have the love, support and nurturing of the family unit.

In today's world, it's a real challenge getting families to stick together. About one of every two marriages ends in divorce, which only perpetuates a vicious cycle in which nobody wins. The parents lose. The children lose. Our country loses.

We need to find a way to break that cycle before it's too late. It's no coincidence that as the breakdown of the family unit has increased, America's strength has decreased. The two go hand in hand.

As I reflect back over my childhood, it's obvious I was blessed with a very strong and supportive family. Mom and Dad instilled strong, Christian values in their children that were passed on to them from their parents.

There's no great secret here. My parents had no special formula for raising their kids that wasn't available to everybody else. It's called hard work. They made a conscious decision in their marriage to put the family first. They built a print shop right next to our house so they could always be there for us.

I believe what's happening in this country is too many people think a strong family unit can be raised by taking shortcuts. Kids often do not get enough structure and discipline at home because parents are either split up or too busy with outside interests. Children want structure. They want discipline. Above all, they want love and a feeling of belonging. If they don't get enough of that at home, they will likely go elsewhere to find it.

Raising families we can all be proud of takes sacrifice and commitment. David Williams, a former offensive tackle with the Houston Oilers, was that team's first-round draft pick in 1989. He was one of the Oilers' most dependable starters, but he received more publicity for one act than anything he ever did on the football field.

Midway through the 1993 season, he came home early from a road trip to New England to be with his wife, Debbie, for the birth of their first child, Scot. Nothing unusual about that decision, except that Williams was docked $111,000 (one game's pay) by the club for missing the game. Still, he made a bigger statement with that gesture than anything he could have done on the field. He put family first.

No foundation in America is more important than the family. Our founding forefathers' vision for a strong, united, morally sound nation cannot be achieved when that unit is broken.

Since the 1960s, we have been attempting to substitute a government system for a family system. As the family unit and responsible parenting decline, the need for policing and government social programs increases. There will never be enough courts and prisons if there are not enough good homes and parents who are willing to make family a priority. It's that simple.

I'm so thankful my parents, and their parents before them, took the time and effort to make our family one that was filled with love and constant support. To be totally honest, I didn't think my parents were always on my side. I mean, can you imagine them having the audacity to not let me hang out with certain kids. To make me be home forty-five minutes after a school night function. To dress a certain way. To not go to particular hangouts.

Strange how the older I get, the smarter Mom and Dad get. No amount of thanks can repay the debt I owe them. The only way I can make it even is to make sure that I put my family first. To make the effort to give my son, Cody, the direction and guidance my parents gave me.

Like this type-written note my Mom left on my bed after we had a little disagreement during my freshman year of high school. It was entitled "Do Yourself a Favor and..."

(1) Stay close to God. Use Him as your guide. He can help you reach your goals better than anyone else.

(2) Be honest with everyone so they can have faith in you.

(3) Use your time wisely; it's always later than you realize (that's nature).

(4) Be a leader for what is right and just and worthwhile.

(5) Be careful of the friends you choose and how they lead you.

(6) Never be ashamed of your family. Someday I think you will realize they were all for you in everything you were involved with.

(7) Be the best possible in all that you do and you'll receive the best results. It is all difficult, but worthwhile. We will always love and care for you, even when you don't think we do.

> Love,
> Mom and Dad

We've filled our day-care centers. We've tied up our juvenile court system. We've watched our kids attempt to find answers in drugs and alcohol. We've even permitted condoms to be passed out in our schools. Perhaps it's time we tried something else.

Giving our children what they deserve—roots and wings.

3

Working Extra Innings

My Mom is what you would call a pack rat. She saves just about everything—stuff that most people wouldn't give a second thought to keeping around. She's got mementos galore, especially things pertaining to the wonder years of her three kids—team pictures, trophies, articles, report cards, 4-H Club ribbons, letters, plaques. Nobody, I mean nobody, does a better job of hanging on to memories.

Among the things Mom kept in boxes for posterity were these grade-school forms she filled out every year. It listed my activities, achievements and teachers for that particular year. One of the categories was "When I grow up, I want to be. . ." and you had to check the appropriate box. I always put a mark beside "baseball player," skipping right over astronaut, policeman, fireman, etc. If something you aspired to be wasn't on there, you had to check the blank box and fill in what you wanted to be.

Starting in third grade at St. Lucie Primary School, and for the years afterward at Saint Anastasia, I also put a check mark in that blank box and wrote beside it: "football player."

While most people identify me with baseball, the truth is, I dreamed of being a successful quarterback as much as anything else. I loved watching Bob Griese and the Miami Dolphins. They were in their glory years when my loyalties were evenly split between football and baseball.

As dedicated as I was in Little League, it was a football experience—the Punt, Pass & Kick competition sponsored by the Ford Motor Company—that first instilled in me the value of practice and attention to detail.

I've been part of high school football pre-season two-a-days in the south Florida summer.

I've been to spring training with the Philadelphia Phillies, New York Mets and Kansas City Royals.

I've been to sports camps for Little League, been named the Most Valuable Player in both the Ray Graves camp at the University of Florida and the Bob Griese camp.

None of those experiences carried as lasting an impact about the importance of practice and mental preparation as Punt, Pass & Kick.

It did more than give me the opportunity to make a name for myself. It taught me that half the battle in sports is learning how to concentrate and to always focus on how you can get better.

A pretty good game plan for life, too.

From age eight to thirteen, I participated in Punt, Pass & Kick, a skills contest that basically turned football into an individual sport. Competitors in their respective age groups were tested on how far they could punt, throw or kick a football with accuracy. They'd stretch out a tape to measure distance, but you were also penalized for how far away from that tape the ball landed.

This competition only comes around once a year, but as a youngster, I don't think I worked so hard in practice at anything. A lot of it goes back to my Mom and Dad's philosophy about doing your best. I guess the reason this made such a big impression on me over time was it was my first taste of notoriety as an athlete.

I won the local competition all six years, and each win entitled a competitor to advance to district, zone, regionals and nationals until he was eliminated. At age ten, I made it to nationals. I won a regional competition at half-time of a Miami Dolphins-Baltimore Colts game in the Orange Bowl (Nov. 22, 1970) and earned an expenses-paid trip to San Diego.

With emphasis on the word *earned,* because it took a lot of concentration and painstaking practice. It taught me the value of sacrificing to reach a goal.

Mom and Dad did their part to help me prepare. Mom shopped all over for a certain type of tennis shoe that had the squarest toe for a straight-on kicker because you weren't allowed to use cleats. One of the problems I had was learning how to run to the ball and kick it straight. Dad helped me by chalking my toe so that I'd see if I was hitting the right spot on the ball.

I showed an interest in kicking a football long before competing in Punt, Pass & Kick or YMCA flag football. In one of Dad's classic examples of thinking ahead, he had this retired machinist he knew build a goal post to put up on the side of our house.

So when I got older, I'd have a head start on kicking extra points and field goals. I've still got a scar on my right leg from the time we put in one of the uprights. I was holding the pole to put it in and this huge iron pipe slipped, catching my leg between two poles, and pinching the crud out of me.

Now, the property where our old house sits wasn't very big. It was sixty-five feet by one-hundred-thirty feet and nearly half of that was occupied by the house and my parents' print shop. Not much room for a regulation-sized goal post, but we managed to squeeze a slightly smaller version between the edge of the house and a fence that separated our yard from the bakery next door.

Dad also had a net put up on a pulley so I could practice on my own, kicking the ball into the net and teeing it back up after I retrieved it. By the time I was fourteen, the net was useless. I'd tee the ball up in front of the print shop, right next to the main highway. It was about forty yards from the goal post and balls would sail over into the street behind our house.

You probably think this is a lot of trouble to go to just to kick a football. But when my parents asked us to do our best, that meant not taking shortcuts. They always did their part, in little and big ways, to help their kids succeed.

Practice, practice, practice. It's not always fun, but it usually pays off.

When it came to Punt, Pass & Kick, other kids thought I was crazy to spend so much time practicing. Sometimes, I'd have to miss out on things because when Dad was done working in the print shop, we'd go to the back yard and practice.

One time when we were vacationing at Black Rock Mountain

in Georgia, we went down the mountain and found a schoolyard where I could work on my kicking and passing. I'm sure there were kids and parents that wondered if Mr. Hearn was pushing his son too hard. I know they did in Little League.

But I honestly believe the discipline I learned from this Punt, Pass & Kick competition helped instill a drive in me that produced long-term benefits.

I think once you become structured and organized in one area, it spills into other aspects of your life. You just can't turn the faucet on and off. If you're sloppy in practice, you're probably going to make careless mistakes in the game.

Punt, Pass & Kick showed me that much. I also learned something else: winning was a lot of fun.

There's nothing like setting a goal to bring out the best in you. I knew how much time I invested in practice, so that made success in the Punt, Pass & Kick competition important.

But you never know when you're going to run into hurdles that you don't count on. I usually breezed through the local competition and won the zone portion in Orlando three times out of those six years.

My biggest mental block was the district competition at the Gator Bowl in Jacksonville. They always made you kick from the sidelines toward the middle of the field and I had never seen a field as sloped as that one was for drainage purposes. This was a huge mental obstacle for me because it made me feel like I was kicking up a mountain.

At that time of year, the competition was held while the annual fair took place near the Gator Bowl. The smell from there was just grotesque. It's ironic when I see what a beautiful facility they've got now in Jacksonville for the NFL Jaguars. Twenty-five years ago, that place was the pits to me.

I remember this so vividly because, psychologically, these little things that shouldn't have been a big deal put negative thoughts in my head. I never performed real well in Jacksonville. I was eliminated two out of the three times there, and not necessarily because the competition was any better. I just had to learn to overcome the mental part of it.

At age ten, I did manage to get over that hump and won the opportunity to compete in my dream setting: the Orange Bowl. Remember, this was 1970, the Dolphins were on the verge of greatness, and it was before that area of Miami became run down. This was big-league stuff.

Think about this from a kid's point of view. How many times is a ten-year-old going to get a chance to compete in front of 75,000 people? I had been to the Orange Bowl many times as a spectator. I used to hang out with Mom and Dad after games waiting for Bob Griese to come out of the locker room.

Because I went to his sports camps, he would always recognize me out of all the kids who gathered around him for autographs. I never went looking for his autograph. He would just stand there and talk to me as he signed all the other kids' stuff. It was like we were old buddies.

Still, nothing could top what I felt competing on the same Orange Bowl turf as my Miami Dolphin heroes—Griese, Karl Noonan, Paul Warfield, Larry Csonka and Norm Evans, a lineman whom I would meet up with again years later in a neat way. I never forgot Norm at Dolphins' training camp because he gave me my first autograph that had a Bible verse next to it.

By half-time of that Dolphins-Colts game, I pretty much knew I was going to win this two-man race. The punting and kicking portion of the program was held before the game and the kid I competed against, Tom Barrows from Fort Lauderdale, slipped as he went to kick the ball and got a real low score.

That put him behind the eight-ball the rest of the way. In my Miami Dolphins uniform, pads and all, I passed the ball a net twenty-one yards in front of a capacity crowd in the Orange Bowl. My final score was 214, not quite up to my scores of 293 and 259 in earlier competitions, but it was good enough to win a free trip to San Diego.

I got my picture in the newspaper and was interviewed by our local television station. I received all kinds of publicity. Jimmy

Sneed, who owned the local Ford dealership, put up a sign that stood out on the main highway through Ft. Pierce. That sign really made me feel good. It said: "Congratulations, Ed Hearn—Punt, Pass and Kick District Champion."

What an awesome feeling! But the best part was yet to come.

It seemed that I mentioned in a TV interview that Ford Motor Co. took care of the expenses for the winner and one parent to go to San Diego. No way could my folks afford a plane ticket out to California, so it was just going to be me and my Dad.

Some people in my hometown were going to attempt to raise the money for Mom to go, then Jimmy Sneed heard about it and he paid Mom's expenses. I'll never forget that gesture because I'd have hated for such a giving and caring person like my Mom to have missed out on something she helped make possible.

This trip was a big deal to us. We got to fly on a big 747 jet and stay in the Hilton Hotel. That was some posh digs, especially when you compared it to the cheap motels we always stayed in on family vacations.

I got beat out in San Diego, finishing fourth out of thirteen national semifinalists, but it was a really neat experience because my parents never got to do anything like that. We spent part of a day in Mexico, too.

For a little while anyway, the Hearns got a taste of the high life. Maybe all that extra practice wasn't so bad after all.

Without Punt, Pass & Kick, I don't think I would have excelled as much as I did in football. The habits that I formed in preparing for that kind of competition set the tone. I knew I had the foundation to be a skill position player, not just evolve into a down lineman because I happened to be bigger than most kids my age.

I played quarterback all the way through YMCA League. The first couple years were flag football with the Chargers, then three years of tackle football for the Kiwanis Club Wildcats, coached by (who else?) my Dad.

One of my best moments came in a game where I was supposed to be strictly a spectator. I had been running a pretty high fever that day, so Dad kept me on the sideline. Then we got down by a couple of touchdowns in the second half and Dad put me in, giving me strict orders to not try anything fancy. Just get the ball to our fastest receiver, Darwin Cain, and let him do the rest. Darwin caught three of my passes and turned them into touchdowns. We pulled it out.

Unfortunately, my football career didn't have many bright moments after my YMCA days. At least not as a quarterback, mostly because of circumstances beyond my control. Part of it was injuries. Part of it was a racist mentality.

When I made the transition from Catholic to public school in eighth grade, I would soon learn how different the ground rules were.

A white catcher at Fort Pierce Central High School was OK. But a white quarterback?

Brother, that wasn't going to fly. Not very smoothly anyway.

The Inside Pitch

Paying the Price

"He is a sorry dog who wants game, but does not want to hunt for it."

Everybody in life wants to be a success. The problem is, not everybody wants to work for it. We want instant gratification. The thought of putting in years of dedicated effort to realize a dream often weighs people down. It keeps them out of the hunt.

I remember back in high school, some of my teammates and friends would sometimes get a case of beer and head for the beach to party. They'd say: "Come on, Ed. We got the beer, the babes are coming down. Let's go." But I was always the stick in the mud. I'd either mention something about a big paper due next week or remind them: "Hey, we've got a game tomorrow." Then they'd give me that look of resignation and tell me how uncool I was.

When I came back to my hometown of Fort Pierce after my first year in the big leagues, I ran into some of these same high school buddies. They were singing a different tune. "Hey, Ed, we saw you playing on national television. Check out that World Series ring! Man, you're so lucky!"

After all those years, they still didn't get it. There's a price to pay for success.

What kind of price are you willing to pay? If the hunt is long and hard, are you willing to stick it out? Can you put up with the distractions and circumstances that may get in the way of reaching your goal?

Over time, I learned I had to take personal responsibility to make things happen in my life. If you don't see an opportunity, then you have to find a way to create it. That's part of the hunt, too. So is doing all the little things necessary to succeed.

Athletic competition, in many ways, is a microcosm of life. Frustration, joy, uncertainty, pain and struggle are all there. People who enter the competitive arena soon realize that there is much more to winning than merely wanting to win.

Having played with and against some of the greatest players in baseball, I have had the opportunity to observe some of these athletes practice a dedicated work ethic that fans never get to see. Hall of Fame basketball player Julius Erving once said: "A lot of people looked at me and they said: 'Gosh, you're the luckiest man to have all that talent.' They didn't see all the years of practice that went into it."

Granted, there are times when some professional athletes seem only to go through the motions. But, one thing I learned from thirteen years in pro ball; great players are never complacent.

One day, early in my first season with the Kansas City Royals, I had arrived at the ball park some seven hours prior to game time. I didn't come in to do any extra work. I was just looking for a quiet place to read the morning paper and get some fresh air.

When I walked into the locker room, I unloaded my duffel bags and headed for the doors leading to the entrance of the dugout. It was a beautiful day, a perfect time to relax without the noise of teammates, reporters or fans being around.

Then suddenly, walking up the dugout steps, the crack of a bat echoing through the stadium startled me. Who could it be that early in the afternoon? At first, I thought one of the bat boys must have skipped school to come out early and have a little fun on the field before all the players arrived. But then, as I looked closer, I saw the number five on a Royals' practice jersey.

And I realized, WOW, it's George Brett. The very same man who only a few years earlier almost became the first player since Ted Williams in 1941 to hit .400 in a single season. This was a thirteen-time All Star player taking batting practice off a tee! Yes, the very same batting tee most of us learned the game with as five-year-olds. The sweat was dripping off Brett's forehead as he kept pounding away, perfecting that swing that made him one of the greatest hitters of all time.

It's a scene I have never forgotten. Here I was, only in my second year in the big leagues, watching this future Hall of Fame player busting his rear end in the afternoon heat without a soul in the ball park. What does this say to you about the value of paying the price? What does this say about always striving to improve yourself?

Albert Gray, the former president of Prudential Insurance Company, wrote a booklet called *The Common Denominator of Success.* In it, he made a point that illustrates why that sight of George Brett taking extra batting practice by himself is so telling.

Gray wrote: "Successful people do the things other people do not like to do. People who do not want to spend time on tasks that are tedious, boring or strenuous are usually people who fail at life."

Joe Louis, the great boxer, put it another way when he said: "Everyone wants to go to heaven, but nobody wants to die."

The hunt for success comes down to this simple point. If you want to soar like an eagle in life, you can't sit around with the pigeons waiting for handouts.

4

Big Man
on Campus?

*E*verybody likes having a comfort zone in life. Just being secure in who you are, what you're doing and believing that your long-term goals will be reached. I transferred out of Catholic school and into the St. Lucie County public school system with my future in mind.

It was a gamble, leaving behind friends at Saint Anastasia and walking into an apprehensive situation at Fort Pierce Central High, but it's a risk I had to take.

In the early 1970s, racial unrest was a big problem in my hometown. Many parents sent their kids to John Carroll High School not only for the private-school education, but to avoid potential confrontations that did occur as a result of mandated desegregation.

Fortunately, by the time I enrolled at Central in 1974, a lot of the tension had subsided. I knew my future prospects for college scholarships or pro ball would improve by playing at the bigger high school. I had watched too many good players go through John Carroll—guys like Dale King, Rick Dixon and his younger brother, John—and not get the kind of opportunities that their talents merited. You just didn't see as many college or pro scouts at John Carroll games. I didn't want to lose out.

So I switched over to public school in eighth grade to become acclimated with future classmates and teammates I'd have at Central. I tried to coax a few athletes into transferring with me, especially Richard Carnell, who I thought had the potential to be a good wide receiver. But his mother wanted him to stay at John Carroll.

Even though I was starting to get the impression my future was in baseball, the idea of being another Bob Griese was still in my blood. I dreamed of slinging passes and scoring touchdowns in Lawnwood Stadium.

Boy, if I only knew the heartache I was in for at Central, I might have stuck to catching and left the Bo Jackson thing to somebody else.

One of sports' great teaching tools is that you learn to deal with disappointment. In my amateur career, there was probably no time more frustrating for me than my first and last years of high school.

I got to Central just as it was expanding to include ninth-graders, so the school went to a split schedule to accommodate all the students. That meant going to school from noon until around 5:30 p.m. Naturally, this posed a conflict as far as playing football and baseball because everybody else in the upper grades was at practice while I was in school.

That's when I started taking up golf. I played on the varsity team as a freshman because I could practice with my other class-mates in the morning before school. You couldn't do that in foot-ball or baseball because of the team-sport concept. It felt weird going almost a whole year without putting on a uniform.

For a brief time, though, it did look like I might get the chance to play varsity football. Because the coaching staff knew I was a good kicker, I was given the opportunity during my physi-cal education period to compete against a senior named Steve Sheppard. This was supposed to be head-to-head competition, particularly for the job of kicking extra-points.

Steve had a stronger leg, but it wasn't even close as far as accu-racy. I clearly won the job. I was pretty fired up about playing for the Cobras, but it became obvious they weren't keen on the idea of a freshman playing varsity football.

I had already been given my game jersey for the season open-er, but I was called into the coach's office the day before and told that Sheppard would be the kicker. I guess Phil Farinella, the head coach, or somebody just didn't want the hassle of having a ninth-grader on the team.

This just blew me away. I mean, isn't the best performer supposed to get the job? It was my first real encounter with the politics of athletics and it didn't sit very well. Little did I know that was nothing compared to the controversy I'd be facing in three more years.

Looking back, I probably should have just played freshman football and competed for the quarterback job. If nothing else, I would have gotten experience and it would have taken my mind off getting cut from the varsity team.

Instead, I blew off football and usually went snook fishing with my Dad or grandfather on the nights the varsity played. I'd listen to the games on the radio and when the Cobras scored a touchdown, I'd root for them to miss the extra point. They often did, and I'd get a good chuckle.

Not that I was a bitter fourteen-year-old kid or anything.

One of the biggest adjustments high school posed for me was simply fitting into a different athletic culture. At Central, nearly all the high-profile positions in major sports, especially in football, were occupied by blacks. It was bad enough that there was lingering racial tension from time to time. I also had to establish myself as an athlete with peers whom I either didn't know very well or had nothing in common with socially.

Baseball wasn't much of a problem. People didn't care about that like they did football. By my sophomore year, I was firmly entrenched as the Cobras' starting catcher, but I started to wonder if I'd ever fulfill my dream of being the varsity quarterback.

As a junior, I broke a twenty-two-year-old school record set by Donnie Porter when I kicked thirty-three extra points in forty attempts.

Still, the record didn't mean very much because I got this strange feeling that race, not performance, was deciding who played quarterback. I played sparingly for two years as a backup behind Jerry Brown.

Central had a great football tradition. It won the Class AAAA state championship in 1971 under Coach Calvin Triplett. It produced NFL-caliber players like Robert Weathers and Dock Luckie, both of whom were teammates and good friends of mine. Weathers went to Arizona State and was drafted by the New England Patriots. Luckie played at Florida and later with the Kansas City Chiefs.

Unfortunately for me, Central also had another tradition—white guys didn't play skill positions, especially quarterback.

I was going to break that tradition if it killed me. You know what? It almost did.

Some segments of the black community in Fort Pierce simply couldn't accept the idea of a white guy as the starting quarterback. In my senior year, things got so bad leading up to the season opener against Boca Raton that Coach Farinella still hadn't told Leon Hill or me who would be starting.

Finally, ten minutes before we took the field, I said: "Who's starting at quarterback?" Farinella hemmed and hawed, then said: "Well, Leon, you play flanker and we'll see how it goes from there."

What the coaching staff didn't know was I had already received two death threats. One came over the phone. Another happened right in the weight room at school. That really floored me, because this black guy was a former teammate who had only been out of school one year.

He was a street-fighter type who was constantly getting into altercations on and off the field. He came up to me, stuck a finger in my face and said: "You walk out on that field as the starting quarterback, you're a dead man."

Yeah, well, nice to see you, too! Thanks for the encouragement.

Honestly, the only thing that made this pressure from the community somewhat bearable is that I had support from many black teammates, guys like Robert Weathers, Willie Lanier and Henry Parish. I resented having to put up with all that racial stuff and the fact that the coaching staff wasn't strong enough to take a stand.

Once that first game at Boca Raton was over—our only loss in the seven games I started at quarterback—things eased up a little bit. But that negative experience stayed with me a long time because it soured what otherwise should have been an enjoyable time in my life.

I just believe that who plays shouldn't be determined by the color of a person's skin. What matters is can you do the job and do you work hard to achieve team-oriented goals?

Nothing about that 1977 football season went right for the Cobras. Weathers injured himself in preseason and tried to come back, only to get hurt again. He was a huge weapon in our predictable, run-oriented offense.

I say predictable because we rarely threw the ball on first or second down. We had no audible system. I could read defenses pretty well, but the coaches insisted on sticking with the play they called.

This was terribly frustrating because so many times I saw things we could do at the line of scrimmage, if only the coaching staff had trusted me enough to try it.

In the seventh game against Martin County, our arch-rivals, my level of exasperation reached a new high. I had completed a nineteen yard pass to my tight end, Brant Schirard, but they were on a safety blitz and one of our backs just let him run right by.

After I released the ball, I was hit from behind by the safety and landed awkwardly on my right shoulder. I stayed in the game for the rest of that series, but when I couldn't even extend my arm to punt the ball, I knew something was wrong. The next day, X-rays revealed a second-degree shoulder separation.

The coaching staff hoped I could return in a couple of weeks, but I wasn't about to jeopardize my baseball season or the chance to play pro ball. No way was I rushing back to play quarterback after all I had been put through.

I had already taken enough for this team. Actually, more than enough. As I later discovered, that football injury was the start of all the shoulder problems that curtailed my major league career.

A major key to any athlete's development, beyond his own talent and ambition, is being surrounded by people willing to go the extra mile for him, especially when things seem to be falling apart.

Besides my family, one man who provided immeasurable help and counsel during a stress-filled senior year was Mike Cobb, my baseball coach at Central. After Dad, he was probably the most influential person in my success before turning pro, and even after I signed the contract.

I'm surprised Cobb was able to raise his left arm after all the extra batting practice he threw to me over the years. No matter how much I asked him to help, he was always willing to give.

Cobb was one of several amateur baseball coaches that I came to really respect for their knowledge and genuine care for their players. Bob Hardman, a math teacher at Central, was another. I played for Hardman in Big Little League after the high school season was over.

I just wish I could have produced better for Cobb in my senior year because it was his first season as head coach. He was the assistant coach before that and several players—myself, Henry Parish and a couple others—petitioned the school's athletic director, Charles Hines, to make him the head coach.

Cobb stuck by me when I was stinking it up at the plate. In the first month of the 1978 baseball season, I practically swung myself out of a pro contract.

Normally, I thrived on pressure situations. The bigger the stakes, the better I performed.

But for some mysterious reason, my hitting went completely south at the most critical time of my amateur career. Early in my senior year, there were probably six to ten major league scouts from different organizations at each of my games. They'd pull out their lawn chairs and stopwatches and jot down notes on their pads.

I can only imagine what they must have been writing in February and March. Probably something like: "Hearn couldn't hit a pitch if it was a softball and you lobbed it to him."

Seriously, I felt I couldn't hit myself out of a wet paper bag. I wasn't producing anywhere near my ability. My shoulder felt fine. So what was the problem?

As a last resort, my Mom suggested that I get my eyes checked. Nothing like a mother's intuition. I found out my eyes had gotten to the point where I needed glasses.

Boom! The hits started coming. I went from hitting about .190 to leading the team with a .342 average, which really wasn't that great for high school. But considering the hole I had dug for myself, I at least finished respectably.

Even though teams were probably more impressed with my catching ability than my hitting, I was worried if I'd even be drafted at all. Almost every scout and cross-checker saw me when I was in that slump.

The scout who watched me more than anyone was Andy Seminick of the Philadelphia Phillies. He was a catcher for Philadelphia on the Whiz Kids team that played in the 1951 World Series. He was also one of the most respected scouts in baseball.

Andy was constantly telling me: "We want you." Even when I'd go to invitation-only tryout camps, he'd pull me off to the side and say: "Don't be looking too good out there."

I remember one game down at Martin County, Andy was there with some other scouts and I struck out three or four times. The problem was I had broken my glasses. I lost a screw and the lens wouldn't stay in, so I had to play without them.

I was bummed, thinking: "There goes my chances to get drafted by the Phillies." Andy shocked my parents when he came up to them after the game and said he was so impressed by my swing and bat speed.

They must have been drafting on potential because it sure wasn't my production. I had six RBI's in a thirty-three game season. Six!

Truthfully, I can't say the glasses were my only problem. I just put too much pressure on myself trying to impress the scouts.

In a class of 550 seniors, I graduated fourth with a 3.96 grade point average. But after focusing so much on being drafted, now I wondered if it was smart to put off signing all those college scholarships.

What would happen if nobody drafted me or I was picked in the thirtieth round? About fifteen schools recruited me in both baseball and football, but I wasn't sure if they'd still have offers waiting so late in the year. Junior college was another option because I could be eligible for the baseball draft the following year.

If nothing else, I could always play the wild card and accept the appointment I had received to West Point. This was a prestigious honor, one that many teachers and people in the community urged me to accept.

I didn't know what to do. Until graduation day, which also happened to be the same day of the Major League Baseball draft, my future was totally in the dark.

The Inside Pitch

Dream Big

"The poorest man is not he who is without a cent,
but he who is without a dream."

Throughout my career, in preparation for every game, I learned to use a mental preparation technique called visualization. For me, this entailed spending time alone thinking about and visualizing the opposing pitcher I was about to face. I would replay in my mind how he liked to pitch me. Then I would visualize myself driving pitch after pitch on a line drive. I found that by doing this, I had a much greater chance of succeeding when the time came to face him in an actual game situation.

In baseball, even the greatest hitters fail almost seventy percent of the time. If I had dwelt on that, the probability of being a success would have been very low. So I, and many other professional athletes, find it extremely useful to visualize success as much as possible.

In the movie, *Star Wars*, Yoda, the guru of all gurus told young Luke Skywalker the value of feeling strongly about what you want: "You've got to feel that you desire it. Feel that you deserve it. Feel that you own it. Then, it will be yours."

Belief is a mighty force and when used properly, it can move individuals to accomplish great things. God has given each of us the choice between living our lives in two ways: positively or negatively. It's a world in which you can achieve your lifetime dreams or you can choose any one of a million excuses why you can't accomplish something.

Someone once commented to Helen Keller that it must be terrible to be blind. She replied, "No. What's terrible is for one to be able to see, but have no vision."

What is your vision? What are your dreams? It is so necessary to have a clear mental image of what you want out of life.

If you were to stop and ask one hundred young people on the

street if they were planning on being a success in life, probably all one hundred would be quick to answer, "Of course!" But, if you were able to follow the lives of these people until they reached the age of sixty-five, statistics tell us that only five of them will attain financial security and only one will be wealthy.

Now don't get me wrong, money or financial independence is not necessarily the true meaning of success. But something is drastically wrong when, in the strongest financial country in the world, only five percent of our population can enjoy the benefits of financial independence.

I feel that one reason this happens is that the negative society we live in often creates a poor self-image. Did you know that by the age of eighteen, the average American child has been told "no" or "you can't do that," some 148,000 times. When you are told these things your whole life, you tend to start believing it.

In 1954, the belief was that a human being could not run a mile in less than four minutes. Then along came Roger Bannister, who broke the four-minute barrier. But here is what is so phenomenal about that achievement. Up to that point, it had never been done in the history of the world and that same month after he did it, several other athletes also ran the mile under four minutes. From that day until now, over 20,000 people have done it, including high school students.

What changed? Gravity? No. Better track conditions? Not exactly. No, the biggest difference was that all those people who broke four minutes after Bannister, now knew it was possible. Because one man did it, they believed they could, too.

Anyone with a poor self-image is doomed to constant failure in all areas of life. The fact is, though, how you feel at any one moment is up to you. No one on this earth can make you feel bad about yourself unless you let them.

No matter what has happened in your life, you are in control of your dreams, goals and aspirations. Once you understand that, use all the ability you have to reach those goals. Then you will have control over your life at a whole new level. Then you will have more joy and passion than you ever dreamed possible.

It's not only important to visualize your success, you must also act on those dreams. George Bernard Shaw once said, "Some people dream of worthy accomplishments, while others stay awake and do them."

All of us, to some extent, live in a stressful environment. We feel pressure, either from the outside or from within ourselves. If we expect to feel the exhilaration of victory, we must accept challenges. For if we don't, as motivational speaker Les Brown says: "We will learn the definition of hell—the person you are now, meeting the person you could have been."

So dream big. More importantly, put your dreams into action.

5

Signing My Life Away

We all have unforgettable moments in our lifetimes, occasions which carry such a big impact that you never have to look up the date. I'll always remember June 6, 1978. It was probably my first major milestone. Not only did I graduate from high school that night, which isn't necessarily a big deal, but I was faced with a decision that would affect the rest of my life.

I had spent most of the day over at my girlfriend Charlene's house because I wanted to get away from the pressure. Major League Baseball held its draft in the afternoon and I didn't want to be sitting by the phone at home, jumping every time it rang and wondering if a scout was on the other end.

Andy Seminick tried to reassure me and my family not to worry, that the Phillies still held me in high regard. But drafts in any sport can be so unpredictable. You never rest easy until you know your name's been called.

Shortly after two o'clock, Dad called to tell me Philadelphia had taken me in the fourth round. I was the 101st player selected.

It was an emotional moment, realizing that all the sacrifices I'd made—the extra batting practice, missing out on social opportunities, setting goals—finally paid off.

I was in a mood to celebrate. That's when Dad gave me a reality check.

He told me to get home because Andy was coming over to start the contract negotiations immediately. Whoa! I had high school graduation in about four hours. Couldn't this wait until tomorrow?

Nope. Andy was on our doorstep by four o'clock. He gave me and my parents a copy of the contract to take to the graduation

---

ceremony, then said he'd be back at the house later that night.

By the time we got to the auditorium, word had spread about me being drafted. I was pretty conspicuous at the ceremony, being the only one of 550 graduates looking over a four-foot long yellow piece of paper. It was full of all the lingo that's in a standard baseball contract.

During graduation, a lot of my classmates were saying things like, "What party are we going to?" and stuff like that. I was totally oblivious to everything. I couldn't tell you who spoke at my graduation. I can't even remember getting my diploma.

All I could think about was I was about to reach my ultimate goal of being a professional baseball player. I was content with that for probably too long in the minor leagues. It took me a while to tell myself, "Hey, this isn't where it's at. I want to get to the majors. This is nothing."

But on that day, just being drafted was everything.

That night, Andy, Dad and I negotiated until three in the morning. I was pretty satisfied with the numbers—a $28,000 signing bonus, $7,500 for education and another $7,500 in incentives for being promoted through the organization. But I just didn't want to sign anything that night.

My parents left the decision totally up to me. They didn't try to sway me one way or the other, but I knew deep down how proud they were about that West Point appointment, especially Mom.

People often came up to them and said: "Surely, Ed's not going to turn that down for baseball?"

The truth is, as honored as I still am to this day that I got that appointment, West Point was strictly an insurance policy in my mind. Maybe if I had been hurt my senior year and jeopardized my baseball future, then West Point would have been a tremendous thing to fall back on.

But after seeing the place—West Point was the only school I visited because I told all the other colleges to wait until after the draft—I just didn't feel real comfortable. The idea of spending four years there, plus another four-year military obligation after that, had little appeal to me.

One thing I paid close attention to at West Point was how they treated the Plebes, the way they broke them down mentally and restructured their thinking. It was discipline at its extreme.

I just didn't want to endure that. I had grown up in a very disciplined environment and I felt it was time for a break.

Being a cadet just was not in my heart. If I had passed up signing with the Phillies, I probably would have gone to junior college so I could be eligible to be drafted the following year. It's a moot point anyway because the morning after graduation, I turned pro.

Two days later, I boarded a plane in Melbourne, Fla. for the three thousand mile trip to Rookie League ball in Helena, Montana.

Being paid to play baseball! Life was never better.

Believe me, I was itching to strike out on my own because—ready or not—I wanted to start calling the shots.

For the longest time, I never understood why Mom and Dad had such a tight rein on me. I didn't mind the constant pressure to do my best in school (I never made a C until twelfth grade) or Dad pushing me like he did to practice, but I did resent a lot of the parameters they put me under in high school.

Except for Charlene, a girl I dated my senior year through 1980, I didn't have what you'd call any real close friends in high school. There was a group of ten or fifteen kids that I kind of hung out with, but the rules were so strict with curfews, it reached the point where I rebelled in a lot of different ways.

I never got radical or anything. I never tried any drugs, and as far as I know, neither did the friends I hung around with. I rarely touched alcohol and didn't smoke. Well, that's not entirely true. There was that time in my sophomore year when the football team went to the Orange Bowl to watch the Dolphins and, on a whim, I lit up this cigar and started puffing away.

Mom and Dad were at the game, but they were on the other side of the stadium. I didn't give it a thought. Well, guess what

Dad saw when he was looking through his binoculars? He didn't make a scene, but he came over and told me how classless this was and to put it out.

It's not like I was a bad kid. I respected my parents. Deep down, I knew their intentions were good and what they were trying to do was ultimately for my benefit. At sixteen and seventeen-years-old, I just wanted some more freedom.

Maybe to stay out later than 11:30 on Friday or Saturday night. Go to a few more parties with friends. It's hard to be Mr. Popular when you can't do the same things as kids in your social circle.

One time, during my junior year, I was dating this girl in the band. We wanted to go out one night and for some reason, my parents said no. She wasn't too happy about it.

My folks were very concerned that girls could ruin my future opportunities, take the focus off my goals. Finally, my Dad took her aside and basically told her the same thing. It was nothing personal against her. That's just how they felt.

In my senior year of high school, I decided that if my parents insisted on being so strict, I'd just find a way to get that freedom when they weren't looking.

I did things I never dreamed of doing before. I took advantage of situations, started cutting classes and letting other people— mostly girls—help me on some tests when I wasn't fully prepared.

Basically, I slid into the trap of being big man on campus. If one of my friends or I had an excuse to get out the front gate to the school, the rest of us would stuff ourselves in the trunk and take off for the day. We usually went to the beach. This happened once a week, depending on the weather or if we had tests to take.

Academically, I didn't get a lot out of my senior year. I goofed off quite a bit. For the first time in my life, I didn't take school seriously.

I'm certainly not proud of these things. I very much regret them. I did not deserve my 3.96 grade point average, but I definitely could have made that grade simply by applying myself in twelfth grade the way I did all the years before that.

As usual, there's a price to pay for taking shortcuts. When I went to junior college during my minor league days, I found myself in a big hole in my math classes because I let things slide so much my senior year.

I'm sure Mom and Dad were very disappointed to learn this stuff. If I knew then what I know now, believe me, I would not have slacked off.

When you're a teenager, you just don't always see things clearly. You don't always see the benefits of a parent's discipline, only what you think you're missing out on.

Mom and Dad did their absolute best to instill in their kids strong moral values. From the time I was little, Mom always made sure to read us Bible stories and encouraged me to read books about professional athletes who were Christians.

I'm glad she did. I'm a better person for it today.

But in high school, I saw it differently. The last thing I ever wanted to be a part of, whenever I didn't do something quite right, was one of my Mom's lectures. I'm serious, I would rather have been beaten than listen to my Mom go on and on with her opinions.

Why go to West Point? In a way, I had my own drill sergeant at home. At least that's the way I saw it sometimes.

Mom and I had some pretty serious, drag-out arguments about different things. Usually, it got to the point where Mom would throw up her hands and say: "I love ya. Someday, you'll understand."

I think I finally do understand.

I'm not saying I totally agree with every restriction that was put on me or that I'll raise my son, Cody, exactly the same way. I'm sure there are some things I'll do differently.

What is important is that Mom and Dad know that I appreciate everything they did and for being the best parents they knew how to be to Debbie, Tom and me.

It's not easy for any parent to raise good kids in today's society, but Mom and Dad worked very hard at it. Not that they made us what we are, but without their support and guidance, I would not be where I am at today.

You know, the older I get, the smarter Mom and Dad become. Funny how things like that start to register when you're on your own and three thousand miles from home.

The Inside Pitch

Risk and Failure

"It is better to be a has-been than a never-was."

Over the years, I have often been asked if I had any regrets signing to play pro ball instead of going on to college. The answer is no. Absolutely none. Sometimes in life we have to stick our necks out and take risks. Sometimes we win, sometimes we lose, but at least we're in the game.

Life is not a spectator sport, yet so many people spend their lives holding back in order to minimize their losses rather than maximizing their gains. The biggest trap that keeps people from taking action is fear—the fear of failure.

What can we do to overcome this paralyzing fear? As my former Kansas City Royals teammate Bo Jackson used to say, "Just Do It." That's right, look your fear in the eye, face-to-face and take action in spite of it. The problem is, so few people are willing to do it.

They don't realize how important taking risk is to achieving success. They don't understand that no matter how many times they might have failed in the past, none of that matters. In fact, they would probably be real surprised to know that the most successful people are the most successful people because they have failed more than anybody else.

Most baseball fans are well aware that Hank Aaron hit an all-time record 755 home runs. Did you also know he struck out over 1,400 times? Before Abraham Lincoln went on to become one of our greatest presidents at age fifty-one, he lost five previous elections for political office and was also rejected for a political appointment.

Two of history's all-time greats took risks and experienced failure. But they also reaped the benefits of taking those risks.

Maybe Charles Kittering said it best, "You will never stub your toe standing still. The faster you go, the more chance there is you will stub your toe, but the more chance you will have of getting somewhere."

One day, as I dumped my equipment into my locker in the visiting club house at Wrigley Field, I looked up and saw the following words scribbled on the back wall: "I am not judged by the number of times I fail, but by the number of times I succeed. And the number of times I succeed is in direct proportion to the number of times I can fail and keep on trying."

I do not know who wrote that or how long it had been there, but I would be willing to bet that whoever wrote it has found much success. We must realize that if we learn from our defeats, then we never really lose. It is strictly a matter of taking your past experience and moving on into the future with a greater knowledge of how to do things better the next time.

Janus, the mythical Roman god of doorways, is an excellent role model for us as we look at handling our past failures. Janus is always pictured as having eyes, nose and mouth on both the front and back of his head. That's because a doorway is both an entrance and an exit. When Janus stands in a doorway, he looks both forward and backward at the same time. The month of January is named for Janus because it marks the end of the old year and the beginning of the new.

That's my point. Janus learns from where he has been, while keeping two of his eyes on where he is going. We may never forget what we cannot erase, but there's no need for us to be disabled by it. We can learn from our past experiences if we're willing to avoid the errors of negative thinking.

In looking back over my life, I often wonder myself if I wasn't a little bit afraid of taking risks, maybe even afraid of failing. But, after facing the health problems I did the last couple of years, I have found myself much more able to "go for it" in situations where I might have backed off before. Sometimes it takes a serious encounter with the reality of our own mortality before we can realize life is too short to run around scared.

The following piece was written by an eighty-five-year-old woman from Kentucky. I think it speaks volumes about the need for us to live life to the fullest and never have to look back and wish we had taken a few more risks. It is entitled:

Make More Mistakes

If I had my life to live over, I'd dare to make more mistakes next time. I'd relax. I'd limber up. I would be sillier than I have this time. I would take fewer things seriously. I would take more chances. I would take more trips. I would climb more mountains and swim more rivers. I would eat more ice cream and less beans. I would perhaps have more actual troubles, but I'd have fewer imaginary ones.

You see, I am one of those people who live sensibly and sanely, hour after hour, day after day. Oh, I've had my moments, and if I had it to do over again, I'd have more of them. In fact, I'd try to have nothing else. Just moments, one after another, instead of living so many years ahead of each day.

I've been one of these persons who never goes anywhere without a thermometer, a hot water bottle, raincoat and a parachute. If I had it to do over again, I would travel lighter than I have.

If I had my life to live over, I would start barefoot earlier in the spring and I would stay that way later in the fall. I would go to more dances. I would ride more merry-go-rounds. I would pick more daisies.

Now, just for the record, I do not recommend living wild and crazy. But sometimes it is better to have gambled and lost than to never have stepped up to the plate.

6

Foam Run Derby

"*A*nd now batting, No. 4, . . . the catcher for the Helena Phillies, . . . Big . . . Ed Hearn!"

That's how I was introduced when I came to the plate in Rookie League ball in Helena, Montana. It made me feel special, as if I was really somebody important. I needed that in 1978 because I was so homesick that summer, I wasn't sure if I'd even get through my first professional season.

I was only gone for two-and-a-half months, but when you're on your own for the first time, it can feel like forever. Fortunately, the people there treated ballplayers like family. Helena (pop. 50,000) never had a pro baseball team until that season and we reaped the benefits of not only being a novelty, but a source of pride for the folks in the state capital.

In my eight years in the minor leagues before joining the New York Mets, I was lucky to be part of some good living situations off the field. None were as crucial to me as the way people in Helena took to this naive, seventeen-year-old stranger.

I felt like some kind of stud on the plane ride over. Though I wasn't much of a drinker, I bellied up to a bar in the Denver airport during a layover and bought myself a bottle of Coors. They didn't even ask for my ID. Back then, Coors wasn't sold east of the Mississippi River, so I decided I'd try it. Hey, this was cool. Maybe I would call some buddies back in Fort Pierce and tell them I had a Coors in Denver.

Later that night, a club official got me at the Helena airport and took me to the Lantern Motel on a road called Last Chance Gulch. Suddenly, I started to feel more apprehension than anything else. Reality was quickly setting in.

This wasn't high school any more, I thought. I'm in pro ball now and many of the players were three or four years older than me. I was the young pup. Would I be overwhelmed? Not just by other pitchers, but at the prospect of trying to adjust to life three thousand miles from home and living on $500-a-month income.

For a little while, I really wasn't sure.

Wednesday, June 14, 1978

Dear Mom and Dad:

Well, I guess this is the minor leagues! You might have dropped off a boy at the airport, but that boy is quickly becoming a man. This is true hell for someone just out of high school. What can I say? I asked for it, so now I've got to go for it.

Many of the guys here have already played a year or two in pro ball. Some even have played three or four years of college ball in some first-class programs. So a lot of them are griping about how tough the minors is and talking about how poor the facilities are. But, they say it gets better once we start playing games. I sure hope so because this is a pain in the tail!

Please make sure you keep the mail coming. It's kind of lonely up here. Tell everyone to write. In the meantime, I'll keep busting my rear. . .

About two weeks into the season, I was about ready to pack it in. Marty Shoemaker, my roommate, was six feet, six inches tall and just about the hardest-throwing pitcher I'd ever seen at that point. We were having this intra-squad game and a batter foul tipped one of Marty's pitches. It caught me right in the groin area.

The ball hit my steel cup so hard, the cup bent. For the next three or four days, I lay there in the motel with ice on my privates. I couldn't walk, I was in such pain. I couldn't go out to eat. I was nauseated most of the time.

My parents' phone bill that week alone was probably a whopper. Man, I was ready to go home.

Friday, June 16, 1978

Dear Mom and Dad:
I just got off the phone with you, but I'm writing anyway.
It really is great to hear from you. I look forward to talking to
everybody all the time. I guess I'm still awfully lonely, but I
think I'm beginning to cope with it better.
I'm really starting to understand why they say this is such
a tough road. It really takes a man to do this kind of stuff. I
guess I'm learning a lot about life and people. It sure is a great
opportunity even if I don't make it in this game. The time I'm
spending up here will help me make it in whatever else I
choose to do in life.
I'm really super appreciative of the way you raised me. I
am starting to see how it's going to pay off in the long run.
Please keep the mail coming. Tell everyone to write. . .

Pretty soon, the pain wasn't so bad and neither was the home-
sickness. Marty and I caught a huge break. There weren't many
apartments available and we ended up staying with a family in
their semi-finished basement. It had a couple of beds, with one little room partitioned off.

It was owned by a young couple, Marcus and Jan Ulland, who
also had a baby girl, Rian. It was a phenomenal situation to get
into.

Marcus had an old, gray, 1950 Chevy pickup truck. It was a
bomb, but more importantly, it was transportation. Marcus let us
use it, so we didn't have to rent a car. It got to be known as the
"Lead Sled" by everyone on the team.

That truck and the Ullands' hospitality made the transition
from living with Mom and Dad to being on our own quite bearable. Rookie ball was no picnic, but things were finally starting to
look up.

Sunday, June 18, 1978

Dear Mom and Dad:
 Well, I've been here a whole week now and I'm beginning to understand things a little better. I'm still young, but I'm working hard and learning everything I can. This pro ball is sure different from anything I've ever been associated with before. I'm beginning to see how in a couple of years, I could be one heck of a ballplayer, but it's going to take a lot of hard work.

 Hey, you wouldn't believe how this town is reacting to our team. During lunch hour, we must have forty or fifty people in the stands watching us practice while they eat. When we walk down the streets, everyone either stares or waves. Everyone! It's really something to be somewhat of a hero.

 I'm not having as much of a problem with loneliness now. But I still think a lot about home. So keep the mail coming. Tell everyone to write. . .

We thought ninety-minute bus rides in high school were a pain on those yellow busses, but the trips through the Pioneer League were unbelievable. We often played in the Canadian province of Alberta, in towns like Lethbridge, Calgary and Medicine Hat. Some of these rides were sixteen hours. I mean, you get in at ten or eleven o'clock in the morning after bussing all night, then go play an afternoon game. Brutal!

Helena was gorgeous. It had a small mountain on one side of town with a capital "H" in huge rocks embedded in the side of the mountain. You could see it out towards center field from Kindrick Legion Field, our home park.

The whole town was fired up about the team. They had lots of promotions. The best one was known as the "Foam Run." There was a part of center field that was completely green, about forty feet wide. Any time a home run was hit into that area, the team would give the fans free beer until the end of that inning.

When I hit my first Foam Run, I was rounding first as I saw the ball go over the fence. When I rounded second base, I was feeling pretty good about myself. Then, the grandstand came into view. Half the people were cheering and the other half were racing out of their seats. I didn't know what the heck was going on.

It didn't dawn on me until I got to the bench that I hit a Foam Run. I had four or five Foam Runs that season, so everybody loved me.

Another promotion which came in real handy was that a local steak house gave you a free twenty-ounce steak for every home run you'd hit at home. I had twelve of them, so I gave out some to the trainers and then to my family when they came up to visit.

Our manager in Helena was Larry Rojas (no relation to Cookie) and I'll never forget our first team meeting. He sat us down in a locker room with forty guys, looked at us and said: "You know, you must work very, very hard to get to the big leagues. Only one, maybe two of you, will get there from this team. That's not many. So who's it going to be?"

It was a ploy to fire us up, but he got his point across. Everybody kind of looked at each other, really wondering who was going to make it. Statistics show that only about six percent of the ballplayers who sign a pro contract ever make it to the majors. That's about one out of twenty. Not very good odds, for sure.

Fortunately, Rojas' prediction for us didn't come true. We had seven guys make it to the big leagues off that Helena team: me, Bob Dernier, Julio Franco, Al Sanchez, Will Culmer (he was a sprinter on the Bahamian Olympic team), George Bell and an infielder we nicknamed "Rhino." You probably know him better as Ryne Sandberg, maybe the most popular Chicago Cub ever, next to Ernie Banks.

Rhino and I shared the team MVP honors. He was voted MVP by the players and I got the nod from the fans. Hey, I hit all those Foam Runs, so what better way for the recipients to repay me than to stuff the ballot box?

Actually, being named MVP caught me totally off guard. They announced it just before game time at our last home game. Fans stood up and cheered. They were going wild for me, but I was too busy to come out and acknowledge the ovation.

A teammate had to come get me. When my name was called out as the fans' MVP, I was sitting on the john!

During my career, I've never been known as much of a home run hitter, but I showed more power in that one season in Helena than any other time. I hit all but one of my thirteen homers at Kindrick Legion Field.

The only home run I had away from Helena was probably the most unforgettable hit in my entire minor league career because of the emotional circumstances surrounding it.

Mom, Dad and Granny had come up on August 1 to see me play. Unfortunately, that coincided with a time when I was in a slump and having them there didn't make things any easier.

For whatever reason, I had trouble playing in front of my family early in my career. It seemed like I always pressed. After a couple days, we got into a little heated discussion in which I basically suggested that it might be better if they went home.

I wanted to do so good for them, but when I bombed, I started to feel like maybe Dad was critiquing me. It led to this tense conversation. Mom and Granny said they didn't come all this way to turn around and go home. Dad wanted to leave only because he didn't want to mess me up.

A day or two later, we were playing the Butte Copper Kings in Butte, Montana. Mom and Granny were in the stands, but Dad told me he wasn't going. About midway through the game, I hit a towering home run to left field. I mean, it was a bomb!

The field in Butte sits in a ravine. Behind the left field fence is a sharp cliff, about thirty or forty feet high. There is a school there and a parking lot that comes up to the end of that cliff.

As I headed toward second base during my home-run trot, I saw this man squatting along a guard rail at the end of that cliff. He had his knees tucked up and his hands clasped together, as if praying. I didn't have time to get a real good look. The batter behind me made the third out, so I had to throw on my catcher's gear and hurry on back out.

I was warming up the pitcher, I looked out toward left field again and, sure enough, it was Dad. He had his handkerchief out and everything, just crying tears of joy.

I got a little emotional myself. I felt terrible about what happened. It was very immature of me to act the way I did toward my parents. It wasn't until I reached the big leagues that I stopped pressing with Mom and Dad around.

But never again did I tell my family to go home. It's part of growing up. If I was going to be a successful pro, I had to learn to perform like no one in the stands mattered.

The last homer I hit came on the night I got the MVP award. It was my last at-bat. There was a house in left field, a two-story shack that was reachable if you really got a hold of one. Occasionally, we'd break a window or two in batting practice.

That final home game, the fans went berserk for me every time I came to the plate, but I couldn't do anything. Then my last time up, I hit that house.

It was an awesome feeling to be able to respond to the crowd like that. The people in Helena treated me like royalty. I had many invitations to dinner at their homes. Sometimes, I'd play ball with their kids. It was just a really neat experience in a family-like atmosphere.

I felt a real bond with those folks. Toward the end of that season, I started to believe that "H" on the side of that mountain stood for Hearn.

My first tour of duty away from home remains one of my best baseball memories, right up there with the World Series because I was young, impressionable and feeling like I had the world by the tail. But in no time at all, I learned what every minor leaguer learns about pro baseball—if you're not healthy, then you're expendable.

The Inside Pitch

Role Models, Heroes or Zeroes

Their little eyes upon you and they're watching night and day.
Their little ears perfectly taping every word you say.
Their little hands are eager to do anything you do.
A little boy or girl who's dreaming of the day they'll be like you.
You're the little fellow's idol, you're the wisest of the wise.
And in his little mind about you no suspicions ever rise.
He believes in you fervently, holds dear to all you say and do.
He will say and do it your way, when he's grown up like you.
Yes, there's a wide-eyed little fellow who believes you're always right.
And his ears are always open and he watches day and night.
You are setting an example every day, in all you say and do.
For the little boy who's waiting to grow up just like you.

Author Unknown

In about three weeks time, I went from a seventeen-year-old high school jock to a homesick minor leaguer to a small-town America hero. My ego was in orbit.

Here I was, just getting adjusted to professional baseball and being out of the home nest. Now kids of all ages were thrusting pens and paper in my face for autographs. Moms wanted me to take pictures with their babies. Dads rose to their feet cheering for another Foam Run.

We all have our own heroes, people that we look up to, people that we want to emulate or that we wish we could be like. Heroes are people who are supposed to inspire us to reach for greater heights in our own lives. But I'm afraid our country has become a nation of false hero-worshippers. We grasp for pieces of the lives of so-called heroes—autographs, photos, memorabilia—without really knowing what we're latching on to.

During the ticker-tape parade celebrating the New York Mets' 1986 World Series championship, I remember lighting up a symbolic victory cigar. I didn't smoke, but on this particular day, I was just trying to be cool. Trying to be like other players who I'd seen do the same following their great triumphs. So I guess I figured that was the thing to do.

Well, it wasn't long before I had been cool long enough. I almost choked to death on that stupid cigar. So I took it out of my mouth and flipped it ever so casually over my shoulder. It landed on the street behind the convertible I was being escorted in with pitcher Sid Fernandez. All of a sudden, out of the corner of my eye, I caught a glimpse of about a dozen people crashing through the police barricades scrambling for my used cigar. These were grown-ups fighting for a smelly souvenir of success.

I'll never forget that incident for as long as I live. What a sad commentary for how little it takes to be recognized as a hero in today's society. Pulitzer Prize-winning writer Robert Penn Warren once wrote: "The celebrity has long since taken the place of heroes. The hero is known for having done something, the celebrity is known for being known. The deed is the mark of the hero. Mention in the gossip column is the mark of the celebrity."

A lot has been written in recent years about the fall of the American athlete as a hero. Unfortunately, in this mega-media, ratings-infested world, dirt and scandal sell. Therefore, the media seems ever so quick to print or report on the athlete who has gone astray. Professional, and even many amateur athletes, like it or not, are very much under the microscope. They are held accountable for their personal lives, maybe even more than that of the political leaders of our country. This is purely a result of the celebrity-worshipping culture in which we live.

I do believe it's time for the athlete to step up to the plate and accept the responsibility of being more than just a celebrity. It really bothers me when I hear or read of a scandal involving an athlete I know children idolize.

But what really gets me stirred up is how some people in our society can rise to celebrity/hero status by intentionally filling the public airwaves with disgusting, demoralizing, distasteful, repulsive, nauseating slime. Case in point, the king of all slime balls, the antonym of all antonyms for the word *role model:* howard stern (this is no typo, his name doesn't deserve to be capitalized).

How can we as a society ever make such a despicable creature into a celebrity? Where are we headed as a nation when filth such as what this New York shock jock spews out on radio and television across America is not only accepted, but widely popular? What does it say about our culture when his vulgar books with loathsome covers are readily available to any youngster walking the malls of America?

Yes, Pete Rose did a little betting in his day, so we keep him out of the Hall of Fame. Fine. But it's about time we put folks like howard stern where they belong—in the Hall of Shame. For if we don't, we will soon live in a world full of the little boys who are waiting to grow up just like howard stern.

I know many of you who read this will question why I stooped to such a level as to even mention stern in this book. Why possibly subject myself to becoming a victim of one of his infamous, mean-spirited, tasteless lampoons? I mean if he can take pot shots at a fallen man like actor Christopher Reeve, who wouldn't he insult in the name of "entertainment?"

Well, I fervently believe that unless we stand up against those evils that are leading this nation down into the gutter, we will forever face the increasing wrath and violence of a morally decaying society. I for one don't want my children to grow up facing a future filled with even greater filth than we live in today.

Now, let's contrast stern with a man I would call a true American hero—Abraham Lincoln. Here's what he said in answering the questions of what caused the moral crisis which led to the Civil War:

> We have been the recipients of the choicest bounties of Heaven; we have been preserved these many years in peace and prosperity; we have grown in numbers, wealth and power as no other nation has ever grown. But we have forgotten God. We have forgotten the gracious hand which preserved us in peace and multiplied and enriched and strengthened us, and we have vainly

imagined in the deceitfulness of our hearts that all those blessings were produced by some superior wisdom and virtue of our own. Intoxicated with unbroken success, we have become too self-suffi- cient to feel the necessity of redeeming and preserving grace, too proud to pray to the God that made us.

I would venture to say that Lincoln will be remembered long after howard stern's little fad has passed. Unfortunately, in the meantime, stern and others like him will continue to willfully influence our nation in a hideously negative way.

With role models like this, turning this country around is going to be a tremendous challenge. But, if we all sit around and wait for the other guy to do something about it, we will never suc- ceed. Yes, I am just one, but sometimes you have to stand for what is right. Even if you have to stand alone.

7

The Phillie Way
(Or No Way)

*T*hings were looking up after Helena. The Phillies sent me to Florida Instructional League in Clearwater, which was an honor because that's where they sent players they considered prospects.

I played in about 30 more games that fall, but I still wasn't able to shake the arm soreness I felt most of that season in Helena. I had a very strong arm when I turned pro, but throughout rookie ball, the Phillies' roving minor league catching instructor—P.J. Carey—made me change my footwork to a totally different set than I learned growing up in those catching clinics with Zack Taylor.

The Phillies told me if I wanted to catch in the big leagues, I had to do it this way. In my opinion, this was totally wrong.

They thought that using this footwork would make things easier, but it didn't fit my style well at all. Everybody has different styles that work for them. Not everybody has success doing it the same way. Sometimes, coaches need to learn not to fix what isn't broken.

Hal McRae, whom I really didn't care much for as a manager, had an extremely sound approach as a hitting instructor. He didn't try to force you to swing the bat or stand in a certain way. Hal allowed you to use what you had instead of changing things just to be changing them.

Not the Phillies. It had to be their way. I think between Carey's insistence on changing my footwork, my old injury from playing football and the constant workouts in Instructional League, it just got to be too much.

Midway through Instructional League, I began to get a dull ache, a spasm-like feeling on the right side of my shoulder. It would happen only at night. I couldn't sleep. I tried ice, heat, anti-inflammatory medication. Finally, they sent me home to fly up to Philadelphia to be examined by the team orthopedist, Dr. Phillip Marone.

On the three-hour drive home, I went to adjust the volume on the radio. As I reached for the dial, I felt my shoulder blade poking out and sticking in the seat. I thought, "Dang, that was weird." It continued to happen every time I raised my arm forward.

In Philadelphia, I had surgery to repair the old shoulder injury from football. They shaved off the end of my collar bone because they thought that was causing all my arm problems.

When I started rehab from the collarbone surgery, I noticed this scapula was still popping out of my back. Apparently, the interns I told never relayed this information to Dr. Marone, which irritated him later when I had to fly back to Philadelphia for more tests.

The diagnosis was that a virus had settled in my shoulder blade. It damaged the long bell nerve that stimulates the muscle contraction, which holds the scapula in place. It would heal eventually, but they couldn't operate. I needed rest. Since it was already close to spring training, they decided I should sit out the entire 1979 season.

It was only the beginning of an injury epidemic that plagued me my entire career. I was pretty bummed. While awaiting surgery, I did receive a letter from Dad (November 5, 1978) that helped put my situation in its proper perspective.

The opening paragraph said: "I hope you are doing fine and that the doctor was able to rebuild your shoulder like it used to be. I hope and pray that you will again have the arm you had as a sophomore and junior in high school, but as you know, God doesn't always let us have things the way we think best. If it is His will for your life to play ball, I am sure He will guide your way."

Some people who observed Dad as a coach might have thought he pushed me too hard. But when times got tough, he was always there to pick me up.

A year without baseball had recharged my batteries. I played sparingly (no catching) at the end of the 1979 Instructional League. By winter time, I got myself in prime shape to re-establish myself as the Phillies' catcher of the future, along with another prospect named Ozzie Virgil.

But in the winter of 1980, a freak injury set me back another half-season. Just before spring training, I was working out with the John Carroll High baseball team in Fort Pierce. I got involved in a practice, intra-squad game and was running from first base to third. I decided to slide, then changed my mind in the middle of it and slid a different way. I landed on my left foot, getting it caught underneath my rear end.

Rick Dixon, the John Carroll coach and a good friend of mine, heard a pop all the way across the field. As I pulled my foot out from underneath my body, I saw a sight that I never want to see again. My left leg was pointing in one direction and my foot was pointing in another. I quickly reached down with both hands and snapped it back into place.

I was so scared about the possibility of facing another major injury. I prayed it wasn't serious, but deep inside, I feared the worst. When X-rays revealed a total dislocation, with severe ligament damage and a broken fibula, I just bawled right there like a baby.

It just devastated me to think I'd be going back to Philadelphia. Back to the operating table. Back into rehab. If God wanted me to play pro ball like Dad wrote in his letter, I thought this was a bizarre way for Him to show me.

My ankle was damaged so badly, I later learned that Dr. Marone told people that I might not even walk normally again, let alone be a catcher. But that was not relayed to me at the time.

That's not uncommon in baseball. The player is often the last one to know.

I missed spring training again, but I did get to experience my first big-league camp by rehabilitating in Clearwater. It was an eye-opener in more ways than one.

One day, I was trudging through the locker room in my shower shoes and birthday suit. I saw Pete Rose sitting in front of his locker and it appeared he was laughing at me. I didn't think much of it. But a few lockers over, I noticed Mike Schmidt and Greg Luzinski were looking my way. So now I was starting to feel a little paranoid. What were these guys who would go on to win the World Series that year gawking at?

I turned to peek over my shoulder and almost died from embarrassment. There she was, the first female reporter I'd ever encountered in a locker room.

Actually, I learned a lot in my short time with the big-leaguers. I got some great tips from Rose, baseball's all-time hits leader. Not on hitting, though.

Some guys were talking about going to the dog tracks after a workout and I had picked up a program that someone left in the clubhouse. I was looking at it and sitting near Rose's locker. He walked over, sat down next to me and said: "Well, who do you like tonight?"

I was like, "Ah. . . . ah. . . . I don't know, Mr. Rose. I've never done this. I like some names."

He pulls up and sits down next to me and says: "Here, let me show you how I do it." He showed me how certain dogs run to the inside and other dogs to the outside, and to bet on heavy dogs in the mud.

I guess if you're going to get advice, get it from the best.

By June, 1980, I got into decent enough shape where I could run again, but I wasn't able to squat and catch. The Phillies sent me to Spartanburg, S.C., their lower Class A team. I played first base and designated hitter.

In my first at-bat, I hit a ball off the left center field wall. My ankle was so bad, I couldn't even round first base to reach second. I ended up hitting .300 in sixty-six games, but what I really didn't know until later was the Phillies never planned on catching me again. They just kept me around because I put up some pretty good offensive numbers.

Still, it was an eventful half-season in other ways. My high school sweetheart, Charlene, and I broke up. The beginning of the end came after a phone call I made to her in which I obviously wasn't thinking straight.

I asked her to marry me one night over the phone, then fifteen minutes later, I started getting jittery. I called her back and said: "Scratch that. I think I jumped the gun a little. Let's put this back on hold."

I had been torn about Charlene for a while. We had talked about the future. She was graduating from high school and had some baton twirling scholarships. She had decided to turn them down and hang around for me.

Selfishly, I wanted her around, but it was also hard to ask her to wait on me. The night I proposed, I was thinking with my heart and not my head. My baseball future was so clouded, it wouldn't have been fair to either one of us to get married.

When I reneged on the proposal, that was the beginning of the end for us.

Actually, that lovers' quarrel was nothing compared to a real fight I got into that season when we played the Greensboro Hornets. When I was with the Mets in '86, we were in a couple of scraps with the Cincinnati Reds and Los Angeles Dodgers. But those altercations couldn't hold a candle to the brawl the Spartanburg Traders had that night with Greensboro, a farm team of the Yankees. Their top player at the time was Don Mattingly.

This was the ugliest fight I've ever seen on a baseball field. We had some testy moments with Greensboro in other games, but nothing like this. I was in the on-deck circle when our batter, Alejandro Sanchez, got beaned. As Sanchez charged the mound, I picked off the first two players and had one in each arm, pinned to the ground. I told them: "Just stay here. We're not doing anything. Just stay here."

Basically, I was following the code of baseball brawls. That is, the principals in the fight are supposed to do the fighting. The rest of the guys charging are either there to pull guys apart or grab hold of somebody else to keep them from diving in and back-stabbing another player.

Well, somebody must have thought I was hurting those two guys because I got kicked real hard in the back of the head. Paul Fryer, our third baseman and my roommate, later told me it was the late Dick Howser's kid who ambushed me. All I know is I became a principal underneath the pile, where a second fight broke out.

This went on for about twenty minutes. In baseball fights, that's an eternity.

It escalated when a pitcher on our team, Rafael Cepeda, helped Sanchez and they pinned the Greensboro catcher to the ground. Another pitcher, Steve Dunnigan, who was charting pitches in the stands, got in the fight with his cowboy boots on. He got a huge fine for getting involved without a uniform on.

Finally, the police had to come in and physically lock Cepeda and Sanchez in our locker room.

When the field cleared, it was my turn to bat. One problem: my glasses got smashed during the brawl. I learned a lesson that night that I would use the rest of my playing career.

If a fight breaks out, put your glasses in a safe place first, and watch out for those cheap-shot artists!

In 1981, I was finally healthy again and did some catching for the Phillies' higher Class A team, the Peninsula Pilots. But I spent more time as the first baseman/designated hitter, just as I did in Spartanburg.

I ended up making the All Star team and was the team MVP (.303, 10 home runs, 44 RBI). It was there that I met Godfrey Smith and his family. Godfrey was a highly successful insurance salesman, a motivational speaker and our team chaplain.

He and his wife had four kids, just a really neat family. Godfrey was one of those Christian brothers who really helped nurture my faith because I was still, shall we say, "on the fence" in my walk with God. I was the chapel leader for our team, outwardly professing my faith and attempting to walk my talk.

But to be honest, I didn't always succeed. Actually, I was one of the most well behaved guys on the team. It's just that I still would, as Paul talks about in the Bible, struggle with sin.

Godfrey was a great influence on me because he was a warm-hearted person. Always upbeat, always expressing affection to everyone. He openly hugged and kissed his family. He hugged guys after chapel meetings and around the ball park. He was just a very caring person. Just from being around Godfrey and his family, it opened my eyes to the benefits of sharing your affection and emotions with those you care about.

We spent many days sailing in front of his house on the Chesapeake Bay. Not only did he teach me how to sail, but more importantly, he taught me a lot about life and how to grow spiritually. He was just the kind of man I needed at that point in my life.

Dave Mitchell, a pitcher from Leesburg, Fla., was my roommate with Peninsula and I have to tell this story about how we went from heroes to goats in one unforgettable 24-hour period.

This was in my days as an amateur prankster, long before I turned pro in the Triple-A International League.

In 1981, we clinched the second-half pennant the night before our last game in Alexandria, Va. We had this huge party at the motel. As you can imagine, nobody was really in the mood to play the next day because we had to travel after the game all the way down to Kinston, N.C. for the playoffs.

So Dave, another teammate, and I, took a cab to the Alexandria ball park while the party was going on. Our plan was to turn the watering systems on and leave them on all night to force a rainout. It was supposed to rain the next day anyway. We were going to try to get the game called early.

A police car was right outside the stadium. We walked by and found the cop asleep inside. So we sneaked into the stadium and Mitchell slid into the groundskeeper's fenced area where they keep all the hoses. We hooked up two big hoses, turned them on in front of home plate so the water was going out toward the mound.

The next morning, the three of us had shirts made that said "Water Hose Gang." Around noon, we started telling our teammates what we did and they were fired up because now, with the washout, we were probably going to get to leave around three or four in the afternoon instead of eleven o'clock at night.

They found the field absolutely soaked, but it was also Fan Appreciation Night. They were giving away a bunch of prizes to fans. We waited at the motel until after four o'clock. The other team called to say batting practice was canceled because some idiots had turned on the hoses on the field, but they were still going to try to play.

What? No way. They actually took vacuum cleaners and sucked water off the field. They threw gas on the infield dirt and lit a fire to try and dry it out. We ended up playing a game that night in two-inch deep mud.

Game time start—ten o'clock! Arrival in Kinston, N.C.—eight in the morning!

The guys were all over us. We were no longer heroes, but the episode was kind of an inspiration.

The movie *Bull Durham* was filmed at a park in the same Carolina League and had a similar scene. For all the grief we took for not getting the rain out, we should have asked for royalties.

By the following spring training in 1982, I lost my sense of humor. Near the end of camp, the Phillies set the roster and I was going back to Peninsula.

That's it. I was bent on quitting baseball right there. I couldn't accept going back for a third straight year of A ball after being team MVP. I was fed up, going home.

As a fitting farewell, or so I thought at the time, I did the most unprofessional thing in my life.

I sneaked into the team laundry room and found this six-inch long screw. I took a long piece of trainers' tape as I cleaned out my locker because I was gonna quit.

On that piece of tape, I wrote "The Philly Way" and took that screw and hung it on my empty locker before going back to the motel.

The reason I put those words on it was because ever since I was with the Phillies, everything they instructed us to do—from wearing shower shoes to running the bases—was called the "Philly Way" of doing things. At that time, I thought the Philly Way was to screw people. I was so mad that day, I wanted to show them up.

Finally, the minor league director called the motel and he was hot. He told me to get my rear end back and get on the plane that day to Peninsula or I would be put on the unrestricted list. That basically means your career is over. You don't play for anybody.

I had no options. I couldn't go back to school right then because the semester had already started, so I changed my mind and reluctantly went back to A ball.

After four weeks in Peninsula, I was smoking the ball all over the ball park. I hit six homers in 76 at-bats, but I still wasn't catching.

I knew I had no shot of getting to the big leagues without catching, so I told them to either play me there or I was going home. I skipped a game and went out to play golf, thinking about my future.

To quit or not to quit? I decided to play one more game, then pack my bags and kiss the game good-bye. Mitchell (my roommate again) was the only one who knew my plans. The game rolled around, I went four-for-four with two doubles and had the game-winning hit. Everybody was happy. High-fives were flying all over the place.

I walked into manager Bill Dancy's office and said: "Bill, I'm done playing. I'm heading home."

They panicked a bit and got on the phone to Philadelphia, then very apologetically said there was nowhere for me to go up the ladder.

For whatever reason, I don't know, something kept me going. I kept playing. A couple of days later, I was called up to Double-A ball in Reading when a catcher got hurt. I spent the rest of the season there, but I only ended up with 135 at-bats and more frustration.

After the season, I wrote the Phillies a two-page letter asking them to please release me. I wasn't going to make it to the big leagues as a first baseman or designated hitter. I wasn't doing them any good and they weren't doing me any good.

At last, Philadelphia gave me my freedom.

The Baltimore Orioles, Atlanta Braves and New York Mets showed interest in me. I ended up signing with the Mets in January 1983, because their minor league director, Steve Schryver, promised me that I'd catch. He didn't say at what level I'd play, but all I wanted was to find out if I could play the position that I had honed my skills at since childhood.

If I couldn't, then it was time to get on with my life.

Compared to where I had been, the next four years with the Mets was like a fairy tale—four championship rings at four different levels in successive seasons. If that's ever been done in baseball history, I guarantee you it hasn't been very often.

Just think, I wanted to quit two or three times.

What if I had hung it up? What if I had let the Phillies put me on that unrestricted list?

Oh, the memories I would have missed out on.

Not being part of those championship teams. Not watching the joy on Mom's and Dad's faces when we celebrated a World Series victory. Not meeting my future wife. Not having my son. Maybe not being alive to tell you this indisputable truth:

The best dream out there is often the one you never give up on.

The Inside Pitch

Perseverance

"In trying times, try not quitting."

John Madden, the NFL analyst for CBS and former head coach of the Oakland Raiders, once said: "The road to easy street goes through the sewer." Could I ever relate to that!

Don't get me wrong, I will always be grateful to the Philadelphia Phillies organization for the opportunity to get my start in professional baseball. But once I had run into a string of bad luck with the injuries, I quickly learned what baseball people meant when they said a player had "gone from being a prospect to a suspect."

After such a wonderful experience my first year with the Helena Phillies, little did I know the challenging, and often demoralizing, times I would face those next three years. For the first time in my life, I would come face to face with a desire to quit. Never before had I wanted to give up on anything, let alone my lifelong dream of playing in the big leagues.

Have you ever felt that your dreams were dead? Though born to fly, it was almost as if someone had clipped your wings? Probably everyone has at one time or another, but we usually think we are the only ones who feel that way. Trust me, we've got lots of company. Every successful person faces many great challenges on the road to the top.

Sometimes it's a matter of patience. Sometimes it's a matter of taking control of a situation and plowing forward, no matter what others might say or think. The key is to understand you will never have a victory without having first gone to battle. As Zig Ziglar puts it: "The difference between a big shot and a little shot is that a big shot's just a little shot that kept on shooting."

A few years back, I read a story about a man that really inspired me. His name was Joseph Strauss, a leader in the field of engineering. Many years ago, he had a vision to build a bridge across the San Francisco Bay. He drew up his plans and for years attempted to obtain funds and public approval. The people he approached told him: "You're crazy! It will collapse in an earthquake. The tides will wash it out to sea."

Time and time again, banks denied him funding. His efforts were continually blocked by government, groups of well-meaning citizens and financial institutions. People who saw his drawings said the bridge would be the worst eye-sore ever created by man; that it would ruin the beauty of San Francisco Bay. Through twenty years of trying, Strauss never wavered until he finally won support during the Great Depression.

As construction began, he was plagued by a new series of logistical and engineering problems. Not to be denied, he plunged forward, inspiring a huge crew of workers to create new solutions and new techniques along the way. Today, the Golden Gate Bridge stands not only as one of the most photographed structures in America, but as a silent testimony to the power of perseverance.

Strauss, like Babe Ruth and so many other baseball greats, just kept swinging. We are all going to strike out from time to time and face major setbacks. We have just got to learn to endure difficult and challenging times because they're coming for all of us. It's just a matter of time.

The ending to the poem *Don't Quit*, says it well: "Often the struggler has given up, when he might have captured the victor's cup; but he learned too late when the night came down, how close he was to that golden crown."

Few people in all of sports have followed the motto to that poem better than Bob Wieland, a medical corpsman who lost both his legs in the Vietnam War when he stepped on a hidden eighty-two millimeter mortar while trying to reach an Army buddy. Wieland, once a professional baseball prospect, was six feet tall and 205 pounds before the catastrophe in June 1969. He shrunk to three feet and eighty-seven pounds.

A tracheotomy was performed so he could breathe. All his blood had to be replenished through transfusions. Wieland had no legs, but his heart and spirit more than made up for the loss.

In his initial attempt at rehabilitation, Wieland could barely lift five pounds in weight training exercises. He didn't give up. Eventually, his daily workouts reaped benefits that almost defy belief. Wieland went from an eighty-seven pound man totally dependent on medical technology to a man who now weighs a robust 221 pounds with ten percent body fat.

Eight years after he lost his legs, he broke the world bantamweight record by lifting 303 pounds in the bench press, bettering the old mark by thirteen pounds. Amazingly, the Amateur Athletic Union never recognized Wieland's record because of a technicality—AAU rules stipulate a competitor must wear shoes.

Wieland protested: "Hey, I'm not even wearing feet!" But the ruling stood.

Still, his incredible story of perseverance hardly ends there. From September 8, 1982, to May 14, 1986, Bob Wieland walked across America—on his hands. He trained for eighteen months, walking over 1,200 miles to prepare for the journey that would require almost five million steps. He planted his hands on thickly padded gloves and moved forward about three feet per swing. He also wore a leather strap across the lower part of his body to protect what was left of his legs.

Starting at Knott's Berry Farm in southern California, Wieland didn't stop until he reached The Wall, otherwise known as the Vietnam Memorial in Washington, D.C. After three years, eight months and six days of walking, he ended up at Wall Twenty-two West, line twenty-seven and the name of Jerome Lubeno, the Army buddy he tried to reach when he stepped on that mortar.

Bob Wieland has overcome his challenges and recaptured the golden crown for one reason. He didn't quit.

8

Ward Catches A Break

I thought nothing could be worse than those last three seasons in the Phillies' organization. All my injury problems, the constant uncertainty, the club giving up on me as a catcher. I would never face a baseball purgatory like that again.

Wrong! The Phillie way didn't seem so bad after my first and only experience with the game in South America. The Mets sent me to Barranquilla, Colombia, for six weeks after the 1983 Instructional League to get more catching time in winter-league ball.

Actually, this assignment was a good indication that the Mets still believed I had a future. But if I had known what those six weeks would be like, I might have said good-bye to baseball right on the spot.

I joined a team called Cafe Allegro in mid-season. It was absolutely one of the most horrifying experiences of my life. I would rather have another kidney transplant than go through that again.

Colombia, unlike other winter-ball leagues in Puerto Rico, Venezuela and the Dominican Republic, didn't have a good reputation. Easy to see why. The place was just wall-to-wall poverty. Everywhere you looked was a negative picture.

People living in cardboard box-like houses, people using and dealing drugs quite openly. Nothing like you would ever see in the States.

I was already tired from the minor league season at Class A Lynchburg, then Instructional League. Those stops were like staying in the Taj Mahal compared to Colombia.

First of all, it was hot as all get-out down there. We lived in a five-story apartment building that barely had running water. You certainly didn't want to drink it and you could hardly take a shower. Our only refuge was the huge swimming pool across the street in an Americanized hotel. Most of the guys hung out there during their free time.

It was a four-team league, but the other teams had much nicer accommodations. One of our road trips was a four-hour ride from Barranquilla to Cartagena. You had to go across this mountain range on an old bus, bouncing along on dusty roads. The driver would speed like crazy on these cliffs as cars were whizzing past from the other direction. It was really wild.

One time in Cartagena, a few of us decided to take in a bull-fight. My Mom always told me that wherever I go in my travels, if I get to see something I may never see again, don't be a cheap-skate. Get the best seats in the house.

So I took her advice. Bad move.

I was on the front row and those bullfights were absolutely the most gory thing I've ever seen. I hunt and fish a lot and I've killed my share of game, but nothing as bloody as this. It was pure animal torture.

They stick in these little arrows and the blood gushes out of these bulls. They wear them down, then finally kill them with a sword after they're just about dead anyway. It was incredibly cruel.

I also saw a bullfighter get gored right in front of me. I thought he was going to die. He was thrown all over that ring. He was bleeding through his pants, but he was a gamer. He stayed in that ring and beat the bull. The people went nuts, throwing flowers out in the big arena.

Americans think New York fans are crazy? Forget Shea Stadium. If you want crazy, go to a bullfight in Colombia.

It wasn't just the language barrier, the lousy food or terrible living conditions that made Colombia such an awful experience. There were plenty of other inconveniences, too.

Making contact with people back home was like trying to get a bill through Congress. There were no phones in the apartment. You had to go to the hotel and getting calls through was often a nightmare.

Just getting out of that place was a challenge. We had all kinds of problems with passports. I'll never forget how joyous I felt when the plane going back home finally landed in Miami and my brother, Tom, picked me up at the airport.

I mean to tell ya, I raced to the McDonald's in that airport. I couldn't wait to chomp down on some American food. I went to order. I looked up at the menu. It was in Spanish! I almost died right there.

My grandmother is a traveling fool. She's eighty-years-old, has a heart condition, but that doesn't stop Granny from seeing the world. Even now, no trip is too long or tiresome for her. She's as spunky and feisty as they come, and probably the biggest Ed Hearn fan of anybody.

When Grandpop was still living, they'd come to watch me play ball two or three times a year. Granny, sometimes more than that. We nicknamed her "Granny Annie" after the girls that would hang around the ball parks looking to meet the players ("Ballpark Annies").

Well, Granny got this crazy notion that she was coming to Colombia for a week to take in some games. I thought my Mom was joking when she told me of Granny's intentions. Of course, Grandpop wasn't crazy about the idea, but he wasn't about to let her go alone.

I begged Mom to tell them not to come. No way did I want my grandparents in this dump. I had a hard enough time there without worrying about how they'd hold up. They came anyway.

Mom told me Granny's response when I pleaded for them to stay home: "No way am I letting my grandson spend the holidays by himself."

True to form, Granny and Grandpop spent nine days with me in Colombia. They went home shortly before Christmas. That day, we had a spaghetti dinner at the apartment of Mike LaValliere, who is still catching in the big leagues. His wife cooked it up for a bunch of the guys.

It made Christmas in this armpit of all places a little more bearable, but not much. The visit was tough on Grandpop, too. He got sick down in Colombia, but he braved the elements just the same.

This is just one example of how dedicated Granny and Grandpop were to their grandkids. They came to more functions involving Debbie, Tom and me than most parents do in a lifetime with their own kids.

When we celebrated our Texas League championship in Jackson in 1984, Granny and Grandpop were right there for the party. Grandpop was in hog heaven, getting champagne poured all over his head and being one of the boys.

I've often bragged to people about Granny's cooking, but it's really the way she cared and nurtured us that makes her special. I can see where my Mom gets it.

As a couple, my grandparents were a hoot to be around. Grandpop wasn't always Mr. Manners. He cussed a lot in just casual conversation, which would aggravate my Mom and Granny to no end, but he meant no harm to anybody.

He was just a character. It was an absolute comedy to watch him play golf. I remember when he first started playing, he'd pick up ball markers on greens and say: "Aw, dang! Who keeps dropping money on the greens?"

But "Panpop," as I called him when I was a little child, was also a man with about the biggest heart of anybody I ever knew. He worked his hands to the bone right up until he passed away five years ago at age eighty-one.

A few years before that, after I had matured and played minor league ball a while, he heard me give a talk somewhere in Fort Pierce. He knew of my Christian faith and later on, while we were fishing, he asked me if I would do the service when he died.

I was honored, of course, but didn't think much of it because I guess I figured he'd live forever. We used to joke about me doing it, but when the time came in December 1990, it was one of the most difficult things for me to get through.

We had a beautiful service for him at Lake Tozour, the lake he dug up himself from the surrounding marshland. He was cremated and we spread his ashes onto the lake following the service. Then my Dad tossed a wreath into the water.

It was a beautiful morning that day. The lake was lit up in bright sunshine and all the waterfowl that Grandpop and my Dad raised were hovering around.

After Dad threw the wreath in, many of the ducks and geese followed that wreath to shore. You couldn't have scripted a more perfect farewell. It's like the birds were saying thank you to Grandpop for the wonderful place he made for them.

I know Grandpop's in a better place today, but I miss that man.

If my son, Cody, ever plays baseball, you can bet that wherever it is, great Granny will be there.

Except for my time in South America, the only eventful thing about that first year with the Mets was the makeup of our squad and the special friends I made in Lynchburg. It was one of the most dominant teams in minor league history. We won 96 of 139 games and captured the Carolina League championship.

Meanwhile, I had a great time making friends with some of the home-towners, especially Mr. Calvin Falwell and a young lady named Susan Amowitz. It's always fun winning, but it's particularly enjoyable when the town is so supportive of the ball club.

It also helps when you have a team that's loaded with a bunch of future major leaguers. Mark Carreon. Calvin Schiraldi. Randy Milligan. Jay Tibbs. I shared the catching duties with Greg Olson, who also made it to "The Bigs." I got off to a typically slow start, but ended up hitting .272 with five homers and forty-seven RBI's.

But the real studs on Lynchburg were Lenny Dykstra and Dwight Gooden, both future All Stars. Lenny was a hitting, base-stealing machine. He batted .358 and stole 105 bases.

Dykstra's nickname, Nails, was rather appropriate. He was a pretty wild, crude guy. Not the kind of person you would want your kid to emulate off the field, but in-between the foul lines, they don't come much more gutsy or competitive.

Gooden was only 18 that year, but I just knew from catching

him that he could punch a ticket to Cooperstown if he stayed healthy and focused. He struck out the last two batters in his final inning that year to get him to three hundred strikeouts.

For a kid his age, he was unbelievable with his velocity, poise and temperament. I never saw anybody as close to dominating as Dwight was. When he had two pitches working, oh, my goodness, it was just hilarious. Guys came into the batter's box beaten before they ever started swinging.

Gooden was the kind of guy you pulled for. He wasn't a prima donna like some stars. He never acted like he was better than everyone else. When he ended up going to drug rehabilitation during 1987 spring training, I was as shocked as anyone.

I can't say I felt the same way about Darryl Strawberry. When it happened to him, nobody was surprised.

Gooden's downfall, I believe, is when he got to the big leagues, he felt he had to do certain things to be one of the guys. He probably succumbed to some peer pressure when he went home to his old neighborhood in Tampa as well.

Dwight and I always had a good pitcher-catcher relationship. I feel bad for what's happened to his career. It could have been so much better, but it's not enough to be blessed with talent. You've got to take what God gives you and have the discipline not to abuse your body or take success for granted.

It's often said that if a minor leaguer can succeed at the Double-A level, then he can make it in The Show. But much of it is luck, too.

You need to catch on with the right team at the right time. So many capable players fall victim to the numbers game.

For the first time in 1984, I started to realize something about myself that I gave very little thought to in six years of pro ball. I had let myself become too content just being a minor league player. I really wasn't aiming my sights high enough, or at least not focusing on getting to the majors.

One season with the Double-A Jackson Mets changed my thinking in a hurry. It was probably the best I've ever played in my life, especially the second half of that year when I went on a torrid streak. I finished with a .312 batting average, eleven home runs and fifty-one RBI's in eighty-six games (splitting the catcher duties again with Olson).

Just to show you how much I struggled in the first half, I remember Mom, Dad and Granny coming out for a few days in June and they ran into the team owner, Con Maloney, while waiting for me to come out of the locker room after a game.

Maloney, who was a state senator and owned a group of appliance stores, was a tremendous owner. He always went the extra mile, doing many little things to make us feel right at home.

Before the Texas league playoffs, Con gave everyone a little pep talk in the clubhouse and passed around these tie clasps that actually had a small clock on top. It was a real watch, and as he passed them out, he said: "OK, boys. It's time to win." That was pretty cool. It got us fired up.

Anyway, when my family met the owner, Maloney started telling them that I'd be a success in life. He said: "Even if it wasn't in baseball, then somewhere else, because he's a fine young man."

When Mom heard that, she cried all the way to the car thinking my career might be over. Remember, I was struggling offensively at that time, and Mom just took what Con said the wrong way. She thought Maloney was implying that I'd do well, but not in baseball.

It's funny, playing ball that first year in Helena, Montana, and that season in Jackson, Miss., were easily my hardest-traveling seasons in the minors. The bus rides in both those leagues are brutal. That can be especially hard on a catcher, but those turned out to be my best years in terms of overall production.

That just goes to show you how just enjoying your work can impact your performance. Baseball in Jackson was really fun, just like it was in rookie league.

I remember the public address announcer, when rain threatened to postpone a game, talked about the "Condome" (referring to the owner, Con). This was the name he gave to a make-believe dome over the stadium. He'd say "We're rolling back the Condome" as the sound of gears grinding played on the loud-speaker. Then he follows by saying, "The Condome is now open and we're ready to play ball."

Fans got a big kick out of that. The people in Jackson had a good time and got behind their Mets.

This one girl, Tammy Hall, and her parents were big fans of mine. They made a scrapbook of the whole season and gave it to me at the end of the year.

Jackson, Miss., was also the birthplace of "Ward" Hearn, the nickname that would stick with me the rest of my career.

That season, I lived in a three-bedroom house with teammates Calvin Schiraldi, Billy Beane and Dwayne Vaughn. I was always cooking and cleaning up. Those guys just left the place a pig sty and I was always getting on them about it.

Finally, it got to be a running joke and they started calling me "Ward" after the father on the old *Leave It To Beaver* show. They'd say: "Aw, come on Ward." "Ease off, Ward." "Cut us some slack, Ward."

Pretty soon, word got around to the rest of the team and "Ward" became more than just a household name.

That was fine with me. I liked "Ward." I still hear it now and then and it brings back good memories. Memories of a time when I finally felt my game coming together.

I was a prospect again. Not a suspect.

Following that 1984 season, I was the one who had leverage for a change. As a minor league free agent, I could shop around and make some decent money after years of scraping to get by.

You would be surprised how many people think minor lea-guers make really good salaries. It's terrible money. I made $1,100 a month in Jackson, then re-signed with the Mets in 1985 for $3,300 a month.

My agents, Ron Shapiro and Michael Maas, who were recom-mended to me by my Double-A manager, Sam Perlazzo, did a great job in the negotiations.

But even with that nice bump in pay, plus the $60,000 I made the next season with the New York Mets and World Series bonus of $86,000, do you know what my average annual salary for thirteen years in baseball turned out to be? I did the math. It's a little over $23,000 per year.

That's an appalling number. To really put the difference in perspective: I was given more meal money for a ten-day road trip with the New York Mets than I made in monthly salary in rookie league.

Is it any wonder minor leaguers are so eager to get to "The Show?"

I was on a 40-man roster for the first time in 1985 and ended up being one of the last guys the Mets cut in spring training. Clint Hurdle beat me out for the backup catcher's job.

When Davey Johnson, the Mets' manager, called me into the office to say they were sending me to their Triple-A club, the Tidewater Tides, I was kind of in tears. I thought for sure I was going to make the club. I had never been sent down in pro ball before and I really felt disappointed.

Davey told me I needed to have a good year in Triple-A, then maybe I would get called up if someone got hurt. But between Greg Olson (later traded to Minnesota Twins), John Gibbons, an upcoming prospect named Barry Lyons and myself, the catching field was still pretty crowded.

I made the best of a pretty good situation in Tidewater, hitting .263 with five homers, fifty-seven RBI's while sharing the catcher's job with Gibbons.

Off the field, I really started to establish myself as a practical joker. In fact, this might have been an MVP (Most Valuable Prankster) year for me.

Minor league seasons can get to be pretty long, drawn-out affairs, so you need to have a little fun. Not go crazy and hurt someone or damage anyone's property. Just every once in a while, do something that keeps everyone loose, but you have to know who you can pick on and who to leave alone.

One of my favorite targets was Kevin Mitchell. On the surface, Kevin didn't look like a guy to be messing with. He's a street-tough kid from San Diego. He's also got arms as thick as the trunk of a redwood tree. He has just a real intimidating look about him, but we were good friends, so he was a natural.

I went offshore fishing for tuna one day with Schiraldi, Gibbons and relief pitcher Joe Graves. We caught a couple of tuna and a big, ol' amberjack. We got back to the dock and the captain asked us us if we wanted the meat filleted out of the fish. We told him, "No, just give it to somebody." But I asked him to cut out the eyes and I took them home in a plastic bag.

The next day, I put little hooks in the eyes and then tied fishing line to them. Then I hung them in Mitchell's locker. He came around that corner to his stall and about had a heart attack.

Another time, I put a dead snake in his shoes and he practically jumped out of his skin. Whenever Kevin was the victim of a prank, he didn't have to ask who did it.

John Cumberland, our pitching coach, was another easy mark. One time, we slipped into the training area and put laundry detergent in a whirlpool tub. Then I took this hose to fill it up so the suds would bubble up all over. I hid inside the tub while another guy stood near it with a coin in his hand, ready to tap the side of the whirlpool when an unsuspecting victim walked in.

Well, Big John had just returned from a luncheon in a shirt and tie. So a couple of players lured him into the training room and said: "Hey, John, come over here, we need to fix this whirlpool." A few seconds later, I heard the coin tap. I rose up out of the suds and hosed him down pretty good.

That wasn't our first water experiment with John. One Sunday morning, after a long night, we didn't have any batting practice. I came to the park and saw John already dressed and sitting in the dugout, but looking a bit worn out. He had been known to have a few drinks on occasion.

So I got a few guys out of the clubhouse and we got this fireman's hose with a nozzle on it. We pulled that thing across me. A couple of guys turned it on and I drilled John right across the chest. He was in a stupor.

The force of the water was so strong, John and that big gut of his couldn't get up. We cracked up laughing.

Now let me say this about John. That big, left-hander could coach pitchers. He was also pretty good at taking a joke.

The end to the 1985 season wasn't very funny for me. I had ruptured a bursa sac in my knee with about a month to go. The swelling was so bad you couldn't even see the bone structure of my knee. I had to slit both sides of my uniform pant leg, just to fit into them. Since there seemed to be no structural damage, I kept playing on it even though I couldn't bend it more than about ninety degrees.

Finally, in a playoff game in Old Orchard Beach, Maine, I slid into second base and the knee blew up again. They had to carry me into the clubhouse. I hobbled into the bathroom and I just snapped. I took one of those pressurized canisters and threw it around the bathroom. I broke some fixtures and a toilet stall.

The Cleveland Indians' farm club billed me $400 for that temper tantrum. I was just so frustrated because, at that moment, I wondered if my career was done.

Fortunately, it was nothing major. The bursa sac just needed some time to heal. I had been on so much aspirin and medications from the first rupture, my blood got real thin and the knee couldn't get any better until I rested.

While I sat out, the Tides won the International League title. Three years. Three rings. Do I hear four?

One more MVP story. This prank may have been my crowning achievement.

That off-season, Schiraldi got married to a girl, named Debbie, whom he met while we played in Jackson, Mississippi. A couple of nights before the wedding, I got Calvin a little inebriated. Then I took the keys to his car and apartment the next morning and had copies made at a hardware store.

Later that day, a couple of teammates and I slipped into his apartment. We found his wedding shoes and put the letters "h" and "e" underneath his left shoe, then "l" and "p" underneath his right shoe.

It was a huge Catholic wedding. When it was time to say the vows, the priest was facing the congregation, while the happy couple knelt at the altar with their backs (and shoes) toward everybody.

Suddenly, you heard a few chuckles, then Calvin's Dad laughed in a real, deep loud voice. The priest had no clue why everyone was cracking up on this solemn occasion.

He couldn't see what everyone else saw—the groom kneeling at the altar with the word "help" on the back of his shoes.

Ward strikes again!

Just for good measure, we put a dozen crickets in his car. I had bought a block of Limburger cheese. I wasn't going to use that, but Dwayne Vaughn couldn't resist and he stuck it on the engine block of the honeymoon car.

Calvin's car stunk like the worst thing you ever smelled in your life. One day, I don't know how, I figured he'd get his revenge.

Thankfully, it wasn't at the 1986 World Series.

The Inside Pitch

Humor Me

"If the world has enough laughter, why are there so
many stand-up comics?"

There is nothing like laughter to change the way we view life. You may have heard the expression, "Angels fly because they take themselves lightly." When we can find humor in day-to-day situations and laugh at ourselves, we begin to lighten our load. It's a small but necessary step toward creating an environment for success.

When I was on the '86 Mets, pitcher Roger McDowell was regarded as one of baseball's great practical jokers. He'd do just about anything for a laugh. He put shoe polish or shaving cream on the receiver end of telephones in the bullpen. Sometimes he put it on the inside lining of a player's hat. In the middle of games, it wasn't uncommon for Roger to disappear into the locker room and come out wearing a Bob Uecker or Ronald Reagan mask. His antics were legendary.

One day before a game, McDowell put on his uniform upside-down. He took his pants and put them on through his arms. He took his shirt and tied it around his legs. Then he went out on to the field—walking on his hands. Everybody in the dugout and stands who saw it busted up laughing.

The '86 Mets won 108 games, one of the most dominant seasons in baseball history. One of the reasons I believe that happened, besides having great talent, is everyone knew how to laugh at themselves. It wasn't a team of robots.

Nobody took offense to being a victim of Roger McDowell's jokes or the barbs that flew back and forth in the clubhouse. Playing in New York, with all the media pressures that can present, you need those light-hearted moments. Everyone should take their work seriously, but it never hurts to leave some room for laughter. There's a reason it's often called the best medicine.

Poet Ralph Waldo Emerson once wrote a poem that posed the question, *How Do You Measure Success?* He told of seven different ways to measure success. The first line of that poem reads: "Laugh often and much."

A story about golfing great Arnold Palmer demonstrates that point. Arnie always had a huge gallery of people following him at tournaments. On one particular day, it was obvious by the look on his face he had lost confidence in his game. He hadn't won a tournament in a long time. He was down and a little dejected.

As he started to set up for his next shot, someone in the crowd yelled: "Hey, Arnie! Charge! You've been holdin' back. You can do it!" Palmer stopped and thought for a moment and then it hit him. He had been holding back. He had not been charging. He had been too tentative.

Palmer took the club and hit a beautiful shot to within a few feet from the pin, then sank the putt for a birdie. He played on a few more holes and was starting to close in on the leaders as the tournament wound down. Once again, as he prepared to hit another shot, he heard the same voice from the crowd holler out: "Hey, Arnie. Charge! You can do it, Arnie. You can do it."

The voice from Arnie's Army, as they called the legion of Palmer fans, was right. He hit a shot that settled on the green and made what proved to be the winning putt. It was a tremendous charge, coming back from a five-stroke deficit on the last nine holes to win the tournament.

At the victory stand, as he was receiving his trophy, that same voice from the crowd yelled: "Way to go, Arnie! I knew you could do it." Palmer turned to the crowd and said, "The voice—who said that?"

A hand went up among the spectators and Palmer wove through the crowd until he reached this person. "Sir", said Palmer, "I heard your voice all day. I want to thank you. You said stuff I knew, but I just needed to hear it. Hey, if there's anything I can do for you, please let me know." The man replied: "Well, there is something you could do for me, Mr. Palmer. You see, I love golf. And my dream has always been to play you in a match—one on one. You give me your best shot. I am kind of a famous golfer myself. My name is Charlie Boswell."

"Charlie Boswell?" Palmer said. "I'm sorry, I have never heard of you." To which Boswell replied: "Well, Mr. Palmer, I'm the International Champion of blind golfers."

Palmer hadn't noticed. He looked down and Charlie Boswell had a cane and he was wearing dark sunglasses so you couldn't see his eyes. He didn't have any eyes. They were blown out in the war on a tank when he went back to save the lives of two fallen comrades. He had been awarded the Congressional Medal of Honor.

Charlie was an inspiration for a lot of people. He was someone special.

Arnie looked at Charlie and he said, "Charlie, if you want to play, I'd be honored to play a round of golf with you." Then, Charlie said, "I want you to know, Arnie, I want your best shot. I want you to play me for $1,000 a hole or we don't play at all."

Now, what do you do if you're Palmer? You don't want to take advantage of a blind guy, but you don't want to show disrespect. Finally, Arnie said: "OK, you're worth it, Charlie. I'll give it my best shot and we'll play for $1,000 a hole. When do you want to play?"

Charlie looked at him, smiled and said, "Any night, Arnie. Any night!"

Charlie Boswell had lost his sight, but he never lost sight of something very important—the ability to laugh at himself.

Laughter is a wonderful emotional release. A good laugh produces honest, wholesome relief. It's an essential ingredient for living a happy and balanced life.

As a fellow once said: "Don't take life too seriously. You're never going to get out alive anyway."

Here I am...only one-year-old and I already have a ball in my hands.

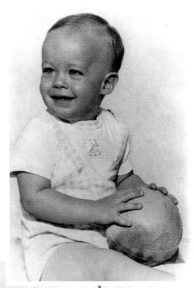

My first Little League team. (I'm in the back row, far right. Dad (L) and coach Phares are in the middle.)

The old high school quarterback days!

Signing my first professional contract with my dad and Andy Seminick.

My first year in Rookie League for the Phillies, Helena, Montana.

Another "Foam Run."

Grandpop and I celebrating the Texas League Championship in Jackson, Mississippi.

Granny and me in the stands of Shea Stadium.

"This one's for you, Dad!" My first major league home run. Father's Day with Dad in the stands.

The sparks fly at home plate, but I manage to make the tag and hang on to the ball.

Ray Knight and George Foster congratulate me after a 3-run homer.

Myself, my childhood hero Johnny Bench and my mentor Gary Carter.

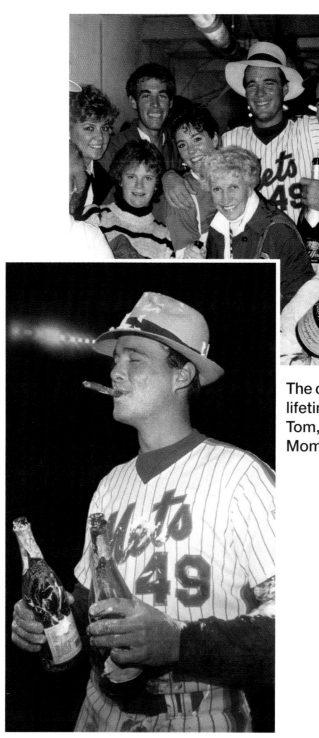

The celebration of a lifetime with Tricia, Tom, Debbie, Dad, Mom and Granny.

The 1986 World Champions ticker tape parade in New York.

Sid Fernandez and I rode together in one of the largest ticker tape parades in history.

The 1986 N.Y. Mets World Series Trophy.

My championship ring on a World Series baseball.

A reception at the White House for the World Champions of baseball. President Ronald Reagan, Howard Johnson, myself, Vice President George Bush and Gary Carter.

Kristen Jacobellis, the sweet little five-year-old with Cystic Fibrosis who would bring Tricia and me together and later be the flower girl in our wedding.

In my new Royals uniform with Tricia.

Kicking back in front of my new locker at Kauffman Stadium.

Determined to make a comeback.

Picture day at Kauffman Stadium.

I must have called the wrong pitch...Carlton Fisk hit another home run!

The catcher of the Royals future?

It looks like Hall of Famer Reggie Jackson is up to trouble behind me.

My proposal from a hot air balloon to Tricia!

Our Wedding Day — November 28, 1987.

Our first family Christmas in Kansas City. My dad and mom (Bill and Jeanne Hearn), my granny and grandpop (Mildred and Jack Tozour), my sister (Debbie), and my wife (Tricia) in back, my mother-in-law and father-in-law (Ursula and Heinz Trienens) my brother (Tom) and my brother-in-law (Thomas Trienens) in front.

A "Royal" debut! Me, Tricia, Cody Carter (8 weeks) and our black lab, Hunter.

Transplant Coordinators, Linda Harte (left) and Brenda Brewer (below) carrying coolers designated for transporting donated organs at St. Luke's Hospital in Kansas City.

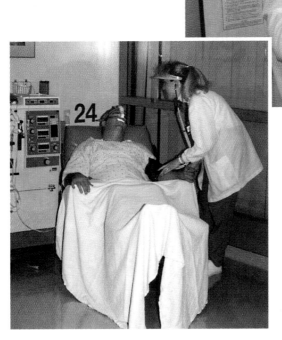

Not one of my better days.

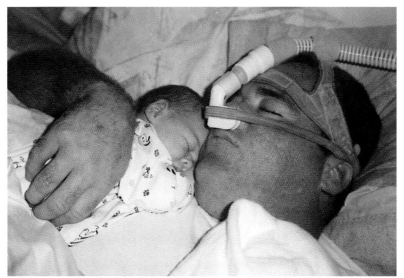

My newborn son naps on my chest while I snooze with my Bi Pap machine on.

Mickey Mantle holding my son Cody at 4 weeks of age.

Caddying for my brother Tom at the Houston Open.

My new passion — professional speaking.

Our family: Ed, Tricia and Cody Carter Hearn (10 months old).

9

N.Y. Bound: Small Fish in a Big Pond

*A*nother spring training. Another race for the backup catcher's job with the New York Mets. Another disappointment.

Eight years of mostly hard time down in the minors had worn on me. I thought for sure my number would come up this time, but Davey Johnson really liked Barry Lyons' bat and that was the difference. So Barry got the call to New York to start the 1986 season while I returned to the Tidewater Tides.

The Mets' plan was to alternate Barry and me, depending on who was performing better, between Triple-A and the big leagues. I didn't find that out until later in the season. When it was time to break camp and my plane ticket said Norfolk, Va., I wondered how much longer I could stand to be put on hold.

Five weeks later, my prayers were answered in a hotel room in Pawtucket, R.I. The Tides were there playing a Triple-A game against the Red Sox farm club. Our manager, Sam Perlazzo, called me into his room on May 8th to say I had been promoted to New York.

It was an emotional moment for both of us because Sam had managed me all three years in the minors. We had some good times together and he knew how long I had waited for this opportunity.

The next night, I was in Shea Stadium in a Mets uniform for a game against the Cincinnati Reds. Mom and Dad came up for that series and the road trip that followed out to the west coast. I did nothing for a week but warm up pitchers and ride the bench. That didn't bother me a bit. At that point, I would rather have sat on the Shea Stadium flag pole than spend another day in the minors.

Whatever happened from here on out, at least I could say I was in The Show.

My first game appearance was anything but ordinary. I thought maybe it would come as a late-inning replacement for Gary Carter. For sure, at home, since the Mets played five games at Shea before I made my first road trip.

I figured they would put a rookie in as low-key a situation as possible to break him in. Instead, I got my first start on the road against the Los Angeles Dodgers on national television in the NBC Game of the Week. Are you kidding me?

That morning, it took a long time for me to settle down. I had breakfast with a friend of mine from high school, Carrie Schwarz. She was a cheerleader at Fort Pierce Central who had moved out to Los Angeles. I barely remember anything we talked about. I was just concerned about performing well in front of millions of television viewers.

The Dodgers beat us 6-2, but I managed not to embarrass myself. In my first at-bat against Bob Welch, I hit a line-drive single to right field. I don't know if I was more thrilled or relieved when I got to first base.

My next time up, NBC announcers Vin Scully and Joe Garagiola talked about how I turned down an appointment to West Point in high school. Scully made note of my size (6-foot-3, 215 pounds) and said: "He would have made an impressive-looking general." Two seconds after he said it, I smoked a ground-rule double to left center. I was batting 1.000 in the big leagues. Look out, Ty Cobb!

I flied out to the warning track and walked in my other plate appearances. Losing the game put a damper on things, but it was nice having Mom and Dad in the stands to see my major league debut.

The next stop on that road trip was San Francisco and I was really touched by what I found at my locker when I arrived. Some 400 people from my hometown of Fort Pierce signed a huge telegram of congratulations for making the New York Mets. Mary Dixon, Carol Gilmore and Ronnie Childress got it started and all these people paid money to have their name put on it.

I guess they don't call it the Big Leagues for nothing.

Once you've gotten a taste of the major league lifestyle, it's easy to get spoiled.

Before we departed for that eleven-game road trip, the team's longest of the season, I received one of the great benefits of leaving minor league life behind—$53-a-day meal allowances. I was just in awe before we boarded the plane and our traveling secretary, Arthur Richman, handed me an envelope that had $650 or $700 in cash. That was two weeks' pay, maybe more, for a lot of minor leaguers.

What I didn't realize is how quickly that meal money can disappear traveling to all these expensive big cities. Most of the players made a lot more than my major league minimum salary of $60,000 and they would eat at these fancy restaurants. Not me. I always looked for McDonald's and other cheap-eating places so I could pocket some of that meal money.

Between that extra cash and income I made doing personal appearances for the Mets, I cashed very few paychecks that season. I just sent money home to my savings account.

The real eye-opener for me on that first road trip, though, was the charter flight. We flew in Triple-A, but it was nothing like this.

I mean, all the rules of standard aviation were out the window. The food was tremendous. You started with shrimp cocktails and all kinds of appetizers neatly arranged on toothpicks. Then you moved on to the main course with things like steak and lobster. I thought I had died and gone to heaven.

What really makes these long flights go fast, though, is the comfort. You actually take the seat in front of you, push it forward, then pull the cushions out and you have a nice recliner. Or, as many of the players did, you could lay the seats down in one row and turn that into a card table.

Charter flights with the '86 Mets were interesting. One or two were legendary, but what I remember most is how the team basically separated itself into three categories—coaches in front of the plane, quiet guys in the middle and the "Scum Bunch" in the back.

I don't say Scum Bunch to demean anybody. That was the

self-proclaimed name that pitchers Doug Sisk and Jessie Orosco gave to the group of players that spent a good part of these charter flights either partying or playing high-stakes card games. It could get pretty wild back there.

Some of those card games went on forever. You would have big hands being played even after we landed. Some guys would be boarding the bus, waiting on players still finishing hands on the plane. The stakes often got real high the last twenty minutes of a flight because guys who were losing wanted a shot at winning their money back.

I got a kick out of the Scum Bunch. It just wasn't my scene. Number one, I did not drink that often. Number two, I could not afford those poker hands that occasionally got into four figures.

Guys like Mookie Wilson, Gary Carter, Tim Teufel, Ray Knight, Kevin Mitchell, Sid Fernandez and myself pretty much stayed away from the back of the plane.

About half the team were Scum Bunch regulars—Orosco, Sisk, Keith Hernandez, Bobby Ojeda, Wally Backman, Danny Heep, Howard Johnson, Lenny Dykstra, Dwight Gooden and Darryl Strawberry (big surprise there, huh?).

They were always rowdy, but one time things did go overboard. The result was like a scene right out of *Animal House*.

Strawberry had bought these filet mignon steaks in Houston and was bringing them back home in a box. Well, Hernandez got into that box and started caressing Strawberry's prized meat. You know, just being goofy. Darryl got irritated and told Keith to stop messing with his steaks.

The scouting report on Keith's arm has always been "strong and deadly accurate." He took that steak and hit Strawberry right in the chest. The next thing you know, guys were grabbing steaks out of that box and throwing them all over the place.

It erupted into a full-fledged food fight, with prime cut steaks as the weapon of choice. I don't think that's what the fans at Shea Stadium had in mind when they started chanting: "Let's Go, Mets!" As the season wore on, everyone could see that there was very little about this team that could be considered ordinary.

New York fans are the greatest when everything is going their way, but let a thing or two go wrong and they'll turn on you in a heartbeat. I learned that immediately in my first home game.

It was a Sunday game against the San Francisco Giants. We just had a six-game winning streak snapped the day before and people were getting their first look at this rookie catcher subbing for Gary Carter. I made only two errors in 49 games that whole season, but I picked that game to make both of them.

By my third at-bat, the fans were all over me. They booed me unmercifully. "Yo, Hearn! Is that E for Ed or Error?"

I had never been really booed before, and certainly not by 50,000 people. The only picture that came to mind was an ostrich. I just wanted to stick my head in the ground.

We lost, 7-3, but it's not like my errors cost us the game. A lot of the New York press interviewed me afterwards and I didn't try to make any excuses. I had a bad game behind the plate and at the plate (hitless in four at-bats). I think the media respected the fact that I stood there and answered their questions as best I could.

I told them I hoped this wasn't the last error I made in the big leagues or I wouldn't be around much longer. They never wrote anything negative and, to this day, I'm appreciative of that.

Two weeks later, I won the fans back. It happened on Father's Day, the second game of a doubleheader against the Pittsburgh Pirates. In my 62-game major league career, this is the moment I cherish the most.

I was batting in the sixth inning with runners at first and third. We were leading 4-3. Cecilio Guante was pitching for the Pirates and all I thought about was getting the ball out of the infield and getting a run home. This was my eighth game and I still had not driven in a run.

On a 1-1 count, he threw me a slider up in the strike zone and I hit it to deep left field. My first thought was at least I got a sacrifice fly, but then I saw the ball sail over the fence. A three-run homer. It was like living a dream.

The fans went nuts. What made it even more special was Mom and Dad had come back up for that weekend series. They were sitting about ten rows up behind home plate. After I crossed the plate and started toward the dugout, I pointed right to Mom and Dad. It was my way of saying thanks for all their hard work and effort, even when that meant giving me a necessary kick in the rear. Without them, I never would have made it to the big leagues.

To top the day off, a security guard came to the clubhouse after the game and gave me the ball. I gave it to Dad and wrote a little thank-you note on it. That ball is still sitting in "Hearnigan's," the name we gave to the third floor of my parents' home where all the memorabilia and trophies are kept.

I also remember that Pirates game for another reason. The home run was my first experience with the curtain call. It had become a custom for fans to keep clapping and standing after a home run until that player came out of the dugout to acknowledge the cheers.

My teammates practically had to push me to the top step of the dugout. I was raised to be a very humble person and to never show up a pitcher, which is how a curtain call was often interpreted by opponents.

But the guys insisted on getting me up there. I must say it felt awfully darn good. You can see for yourself. That's the picture on the cover of this book.

One thing about playing in New York, especially when you have the success the Mets had in '86, the perks and celebrity status players gain never ceases to amaze me.

Even a scrub like me got the star treatment from both strangers and David Letterman.

I was out fishing one night on the Long Island Sound and couldn't catch any live bait, so I just cruised down to LaGuardia Airport, but on the way back home I ran out of gas. Here it was the middle of the night and I was stuck out at sea on this sixteen-foot Boston Whaler I had borrowed from some friends.

The boat had a CB radio and I started flipping around the channels. I broke in on a conversation with some guys in Connecticut, which is across the Sound on the north side of Long

Island. I told them I was Ed Hearn, a catcher for the Mets, but they didn't believe me. So they started quizzing me on stuff about the Mets that only an insider would know and I finally won them over.

They got all excited and called the Coast Guard for me. I finally was rescued after a long night, but who knows how long I would have sat there if I had been Joe Smith from Brooklyn instead of someone playing on a team that won 108 regular-season games.

The Letterman thing was absolutely hilarious. I still to this day would like to know whether it was his idea or somebody on his staff, but it's the best laugh I ever had at my own expense.

In mid-July, Letterman told his audience that books on the New York Mets were just saturating the market, which was true. Gary Carter, Keith Hernandez and Davey Johnson all did books on the 1985 season and Tim McCarver, one of our announcers, was in the process of doing another.

So Letterman followed up by showing his audience the next Mets' book due out, and there was my picture on national television. It was on a make-believe book called *Ed! The Ed Hearn Story*, which Letterman said "details all twelve of Ed's major league hits."

Thanks, Dave. As if my new teammates didn't already have enough material to razz this rookie about.

New York and I really didn't fit. Everything was just too fast-paced for this Florida country boy. I was more concerned about adjusting to the big-city lifestyle than adjusting to big-league pitchers.

Had it not been for the hospitality of Dr. Kelly Mirchel, a dentist in Port Washington, and his wife, Eileen, I wouldn't have been a happy camper. I needed a place to live after staying temporarily with the McDowells—Roger and his wife—then with another pitcher, Rick Aguilera.

The Mirchels, whom I met through a mutual friend down in Florida, offered to let me stay for free in an upstairs apartment above a home that belonged to Eileen's parents. I gave them five hundred dollars a month, which was still ridiculously low.

It was a godsend. Not because of the money I saved, but the opportunity it gave me to do my own thing. On the Mets, I didn't have anybody to really hang out with. It's not that I disliked any of my teammates, but most of them were either married with kids or just ran in different social circles.

What the Mirchels did was provide me with everything this country boy needed to survive—a fishing boat and an extended family.

Kelly and I fished for blues and stripers a few times along the Long Island Sound, but he eventually let me use his boat any time I wanted. He docked the boat behind one of Long Island's best seafood restaurants, Louie's, and that place became my hangout.

I spent many days and nights after a ballgame fishing on that Boston Whaler. Sometimes by myself, sometimes with Kelly, sometimes with a teammate (Doug Sisk, usually). I would get to Louie's early in the morning and if I came back with some fish, they filleted them up for me and I had a nice meal. The owners, Dick and Diane Zwirlein, really took care of me.

When I was out on that boat or just chillin' at Louie's, it didn't feel like I was living in New York at all. It felt more like home. It was a nice change of pace from the wild, exhilarating ride of being on the '86 Mets.

My biggest break with the Mets came at the expense of a teammate who supported me the most, Gary Carter. He suffered a partial ligament tear in his left thumb on August 16th while playing first base against the St. Louis Cardinals.

The Mets placed him on the fifteen-day disabled list, which placed me right on the firing line.

What anonymity I had left was gone. Now I had to prove myself as the starting catcher. Replacing a proven veteran like "The Kid," as Carter was known, was a little scary with the New York media looking for a fresh story and eyeing your every move.

But it was critical for me to not dwell on the pressure and focus on the opportunity it presented. Finally, if only for a two-week period, this was a chance to show Davey Johnson and our pitching staff that I could take command on the field.

I often said during Carter's absence that "this was my team now." I didn't say it out of disrespect to The Kid. I said it because when you're trying to establish yourself in any occupation, half the battle is believing that you're the best person for the job.

How could I rightfully consider myself a part of the '86 Mets, a brash team that reveled in its swaggering image, without feeling I could be the number one catcher?

We didn't miss a beat with Carter on the sidelines, winning eight of the eleven games I started behind the plate. Our lead went from sixteen games when he left to nineteen games on the day he returned.

If nothing else, the Mets learned that losing The Kid wasn't as big a disaster as some initially feared. Maybe somebody would think enough of my performance to consider me as their starting catcher.

On August 31, my final start before Carter returned, I got into a pretty good duel with Dodgers pitcher Fernando Valenzuela. He kept pitching me real hard inside and just muscled me to death. He struck me out once and made me look bad the other time.

Next time up, I told myself that if he comes inside again, I'm going to bust him. Sure enough, the first pitch was inside and I jacked it out of the park for my fourth home run.

Little did I know it would be my last big-league homer.

We clinched the division title on September 17, but I probably scored what would ultimately be my greatest victory about a week earlier.

Earlier in the month, relief pitcher Randy Niemann tried to set me up with a nurse who had become friends with his wife while she had given birth. He suggested I come to the hospital and meet this girl, but I passed it up, having been unimpressed with the few girls I had dated in New York.

A few days later, third baseman Ray Knight, who was the honorary chairperson for the Cystic Fibrosis chapter in New York, was attending a luncheon at Shea Stadium for this charity and promised to bring some players. Unfortunately, nobody would commit to come, and I told Ray I couldn't go because I had a speaking engagement with a group of Little Leaguers a half-hour before this luncheon.

The day of the luncheon, I got back from speaking earlier than I expected and decided to go up to the Stadium Club to help out Ray. He was glad to see me.

A group of kids with Cystic Fibrosis were there, including this five-year-old girl named Kristen. She immediately hopped up on my lap and started talking to me. A few minutes later, her mom passed me an old Mets game ticket and asked me to sign it, and address it "To Tricia."

I obliged, then Kristen's mom tells me I may know this girl Tricia. It turns out she was the nurse that Randy Niemann tried to set me up with. Wow, what a coincidence!

This really aroused my curiosity, so I proceeded to ask Kristen's mom and dad for a scouting report on this gal. As they began to rave about their nurse friend, Kristen quickly chimed in, "Mommy is always telling Daddy that he can look, but he can't touch!"

After hearing that line coming from a five-year-old, I thought, "What the heck?" I called her that night and the next day we went out to lunch. A little less than a year later, Tricia Trienens agreed to become Mrs. Ed Hearn. At our wedding, Kristen served as the flower girl.

The Inside Pitch

Serving Others

"You can have everything in life you want,
if you just help enough other people get what they want."

Zig Ziglar

No doubt, meeting Tricia was the luckiest thing that has ever happened to me. The important thing to realize is I would have never had the chance if I had chosen to go back home after my appearance with the Little Leaguers. Instead, I decided to help out a teammate in a pinch.

"Become part of someone else's miracle, and it will come back to you." The words of this old proverb have become so real to me in the past few years. It almost never fails.

The minute you reach out to someone in need, the blessings seem to start rolling in. OK, maybe everyone isn't going to meet the man or woman of their dreams. The blessings come in so many different forms, sometimes in ways we don't even realize.

In 1987, I was sent back from Yankee Stadium to Kansas City to have the X-rays which would eventually reveal the seriousness of the shoulder injury that ended my career. As I sat waiting for the results of those tests, I found myself really beginning to worry about my future as a pro baseball player. Then I began to think about just days earlier when I had visited some critically ill patients in a nearby children's hospital.

I had gone there with the purpose of lifting their spirits, but I walked away having my own lifted. I was deeply touched by each of them. Yes, the kids had a great time. We laughed and joked and I told a lot of baseball stories and signed autographs.

But in the end, it was me who benefited the most from our time together. That day I visited a young boy, bald from the effects of chemotherapy; a young girl paralyzed from the neck down because of a recent car accident; and two sisters, one who had just

---

141

given bone marrow to the other.

As I sat facing the possibility of a career-ending injury, I would be lying if I said I wasn't preoccupied by the thought of baseball being over for me. The more I thought about those kids, it made my situation a whole lot easier to deal with.

It's true, there is no exercise better for the heart than reaching out and lifting people up. Nothing will lift a person's spirit and sense of purpose more than doing things to help those around you. When you do things for other people, professionally or personally, neat things just seem to happen.

The idea of serving others isn't helping someone in hopes that you'll get something in return. It has to be an attitude that you carry wherever you go.

Three years ago, I spoke to a group at the Fellowship of Christian Athletes national headquarters in Kansas City. A young lady came up to me afterwards, telling me her mother-in-law had just had a kidney transplant a week ago. "Would you mind autographing your picture for her? She is a huge baseball fan." I gladly obliged.

As we continued to talk, I asked her: "Do you think your mother-in-law in New Jersey would enjoy a phone call from me?" Her eyes lit up. She gave me the number.

The next day, I called Judy at the hospital where she had the kidney transplant. She was ecstatic. She couldn't believe that a former major league baseball player had called, especially one who also had a kidney transplant. Once we got past the excitement of my call, she had a million questions about my transplantation and some of the things she might face in the future.

For the next year and a half, Judy either called or wrote to me almost every month. I, on the other hand, did not correspond as often with my busy schedule. Not once during this time had we ever met in person.

In July 1994, I received a phone call from Judy saying she had recalled that I was in the insurance business. She and her husband wanted to make a charitable bequest of $500,000 to each of their former colleges. They learned that they could do this without disinheriting their children by replacing it with a one million dollar insurance policy. Judy asked me to do the transaction.

The following January, I received a commission check for $30,000. All because, two years earlier, I made a phone call to someone because I thought I could bring a little cheer into her life. I had absolutely no idea that one day, we would complete a business deal together. As it turned out, that commission check came at a time when Tricia and I really needed a financial boost.

You see, it is true, you can have everything in life you want if you just help enough other people get what they want.

I once heard the master storyteller, Zig Ziglar, share a fictional story which illustrates this concept perfectly. The story goes that a man was being given a chance to look at both heaven and hell so he could make a decision as to which place he really wanted to go. The first stop on his guided tour was the halls of hell. As he walked in, he thought to himself, "Boy, now if this is hell, this is for me!"

There were a large number of people seated at a very long banquet table. On the banquet table, they had every kind of food you could possibly imagine. They had all the vegetables, all the salads, all the meats, all the entrees, all the desserts. Every exotic food in the world today was on that table.

But as the man looked at the people who were in hell, he noticed that even though there was a feast in front of them, they appeared to be starved. In fact, there was no laughter. There was no cheer. Nobody was having any fun at all. Yet, right in front of them, was a feast fit for royalty.

Then, the tour guide took him up into heaven. He walked in and saw an identical scene. Heaven had the same long banquet table, the same attractive foods, the same menu that he had seen in hell.

However, there was one noticeable difference. All the people were laughing, singing and having a marvelous time. They were well-fed and happy.

The visitor turned to his tour guide and said: "I'm a little puzzled. I could not help but notice that they had the same menu, the same food as in the other place. But down there, they were starving. Up here, they're having a wonderful time. What on earth is the difference?"

The tour guide replied: "Well, had you looked very carefully, you would have noticed that in both places there is a knife and a fork strapped to the arms of each one of the residents. The knife and the fork are both four feet long. Down in hell, they are all trying to feed themselves. But they cannot. In heaven, everyone is fed because they're feeding the person directly across the table. In turn, that other person is feeding them."

Selfishness gets us nowhere. When we serve others, the rewards are unlimited.

10

Never "Shea" Die

*A*fter an eight-and-a-half year struggle through the minors, after the constant struggle of fighting through injuries and other hardships to reach the big leagues, I made a rookie mistake when the '86 Mets were involved in one of the most dramatic post-seasons in baseball history.

It was just about over and I had never paused for one second to just enjoy being there, to soak it all in.

So when the Boston Red Sox were one out away from winning the championship in game six of the World Series, leading 5-3 in the bottom of the tenth inning with the bases empty, I told myself: "Now don't get up and walk back into the clubhouse like everybody else. We're probably gonna lose here, but it's still something special to be here. Stay and watch the Red Sox celebrate because, really, how many World Series do you get to be in?"

Actually, I never set foot on the field during that post-season because we had only two catchers on the roster. If I had gone in to play for Gary Carter, then gotten hurt somehow, we did not have anybody else to put behind the plate.

All I could do was watch, worry and wish there was a way to pull this thing out.

The situation was pretty hopeless, and for me, ironic. One of my best friends in baseball, Calvin Schiraldi, a former minor league teammate in Tidewater and Jackson, was standing on the mound at Shea Stadium, ready to end our dream season and Boston's sixty-eight years without a World Series crown.

The Mets had traded Schiraldi to Boston earlier in the year and it was looking like that deal might come back to haunt us.

You could see the look of resignation in the faces of our players on the bench and the wives behind the screen. Keith

Hernandez, who made the second out in the tenth inning, could not bear to watch and went back into the clubhouse. Everybody was on the top step of the Red Sox dugout, getting ready to charge out and mob Calvin on the mound.

Painful as it might be, I intended to keep sitting in our dugout and watch the Red Sox go crazy.

Then one hit led to another, and another, and. . . . Well, I guess I should have known from what happened in Houston to never count the Mets out of anything.

Playing the Houston Astros in the National League Championship Series made for an emotionally charged atmosphere because of what happened on our last trip there in July. A group of the Mets players went to a bar called Cooter's Executive Games and Burgers during a weekend series, but I ended up leaving forty-five minutes before all the excitement started.

Tim Teufel, a utility infielder and one of our most mild-mannered guys, tried to leave with a beer in his hand. That led to a confrontation with some security cops. When Teufel was ordered back inside, that's when it got ugly. Three of our pitchers—Rick Aguilera, Bobby Ojeda and Ron Darling—tried to intercede when the cops got a little rough with Teufel. Next thing you know, a fight broke out.

Everybody has their own version of how this escalated into a brawl, but the bottom line was those four guys got arrested for fighting with off-duty cops and were thrown in jail.

The next day, being the loose, good-natured teammates we were, we could not resist giving them a reminder of their time in the slammer. Roger McDowell, one of baseball's great pranksters, myself and a few others got to the park early and taped each of their lockers vertically with about five or six strips of black tape. We put a bar of soap, shaving cream and cigarettes and set them inside the locker to make it look like a jail cell.

When the released prisoners came to their lockers, we all busted up laughing. All except for Teufel. His face was swollen and I'm sure he was embarrassed that he got put in that situation. Anyway, he was the only one who was not amused by our interior decorating.

You can just imagine how we were received in Houston at playoff time. The papers there resurrected the bar incident, which only added to the intense atmosphere. All year long, teams despised us because the Mets were perceived as a cocky, arrogant bunch. I guess when you've won 108 games, done all those curtain calls and gotten into brawls with cops, it was an image pretty hard to erase.

It didn't take long for controversy to become a permanent fixture in the series, but the focal point this time was not one of our pitchers. It was Mike Scott, the Astros' ace. Scott had the lowest ERA (2.22) in the National League that year, but the rumor going around was that he gave himself an edge by doctoring the baseball.

When Scott beat us 1-0 and struck out fifteen batters in the opening game at the Astrodome, our guys really started smelling a rat. Scott's pitches moved a little too good. But without proof, what can you do?

We regrouped to win the next two games, taking game three on Lenny Dykstra's dramatic two-run homer in the ninth inning for a 6-5 victory. That meant we had to face Scott again in game four. This time, all of us were keeping a closer eye on his mound routine.

My brother, Tom, told me he watched the first game and continuously replayed in slow motion what Scott would do every time a new ball was put in play. He told me that Scott would take his glove off, put the ball in his left hand and just grind it in one spot. It was not like he was spinning the ball and rubbing it like most pitchers do when they get a new one.

About the third inning in game four, I decided to do a little investigating. Since we were playing at home, our ball boy had collected all the balls the umpire had thrown out of play and put them in a bag. So I just went through that bag.

Sure enough, every ball that came in while Scott was pitching had a scuff mark the size of a half-dollar in the same spot. It was so blatantly obvious. We collected about two dozen balls. I showed them to Keith Hernandez and then he brought it to Davey Johnson's attention. We sent those balls to National League president Chub Feeney, who later said there was nothing wrong with them.

Mike Scott was not scuffing the balls. Yeah, right. I think Feeney knew what was going on, but he did not want the controversy of making that kind of accusation in a league playoff.

In my opinion, there was absolutely no way in the world that Scott was not doctoring the baseball. I've still got one of those balls at home. You can see and judge for yourself.

Throughout game six of that playoff series, the sight of Mike Scott sitting in that dugout haunted us. Scott, who had beaten us twice, had a psychological edge on the Mets and our guys knew it. The last thing we wanted was to face him again in a seventh and deciding game, so we needed to finish off the Astros. We won game five on Gary Carter's twelfth-inning single to take a 3-2 lead.

Game six was easily the most nerve-racking game I have ever witnessed. I wish I could have played in it just to work off all the nervous energy. In all my baseball years, no game came close to being this excruciating.

By the ninth inning, you could not hear yourself think in the Astrodome. Mom and Dad had to scream into each other's ear just to communicate. We were down 3-0 and the park was absolutely rocking. It's one of those dumb stadiums because the sound just echoes right back down at you. I don't know how the football players can hear the audibles from the quarterback.

We finally got to their starter, Bob Knepper, for a couple runs in the top of the ninth before manager Hal Lanier brought in closer Dave Smith. He walked two batters to load the bases and Ray Knight followed with a game-tying sacrifice fly.

It stayed that way until the fourteenth inning when Backman's single scored Darryl Strawberry to put us up, 4-3. We were two outs from going to the World Series when Billy Hatcher murdered a 3-2 fast ball from Jesse Orosco to tie it up again.

When Hatcher hit that bomb, the crowd went bonkers. At that point, you just felt like you were in a forest with a bunch of bees giving chase. You just could not get away from them.

It looked like it was all over in the sixteenth inning when we scored three runs to take a 7-4 lead, but the Astros came back again. They scored two runs and had the tying run at second, but Orosco got Kevin Bass to chase a 3-2 slider in the dirt for the final out.

Finally, we were in the World Series. I was pooped after that game, just emotionally spent. I can't imagine how Carter must have felt catching all 16 innings.

The plane ride home was one incredibly wild party. There was a lot of rowdiness and people shouting "Let's Go Mets!" in the aisles, but the Scum Bunch were conspicuously quiet. The truth of the matter is the players were too worn out to do much celebrating.

But the players' wives were anything but mellow. They trashed the back part of that plane. There was torn upholstery, broken seats, beer spilled everywhere.

It got so rowdy that two days later, we each had a note on our locker from United Airlines saying they would never charter us again. The airline presented a $7,500 bill to the club for damages. Davey Johnson was really irritated, more so at management because he was not consulted before the front-office reprimanded us.

We should have been fired up about playing in the World Series, but I think the emotional letdown after the playoffs really caught us in a funk. We lost the first two games at home and looked awful doing it. Bruce Hurst shut us out, 1-0, in the opener and when Davey Johnson tried shuffling the lineup for game two, it backfired in an even more embarrassing 9-3 defeat.

Only one team, the 1985 Kansas City Royals, had ever lost the first two games at home and won the Series.

On the day off in Boston before game three, Keith Hernandez and Johnson got together at the hotel and decided to cancel the workout at Fenway Park. The Boston media went nuts over that, but it was really one of the best moves Davey made all year and it really made a difference.

We needed the rest, and the break away from the intense media scrutiny did us a lot of good. Our bats came alive the next two nights. We won 7-1 and 6-2 to even the Series, but the Red Sox knocked Dwight Gooden out early for the second time in game five. Boston won 4-2 to put us on the brink of elimination.

It was the bottom of the tenth inning in game six. The Red Sox had gotten two runs in the top half to go ahead, 5-3, and Schiraldi was about to slam the door shut. One more out and we were history.

All game long I had been looking for a lucky spot to sit in, but nothing really worked. Now I was on the far end of the bench, sitting on the next-to-the-top step when Gary Carter singles to left to keep us alive. I decided to stay right there.

Pinch-hitter Kevin Mitchell followed with another single. No way was I budging now. When Ray Knight's single brought Carter home to make it 5-4, I rushed up to congratulate Gary, then hurried right back to that same spot.

As superstitious as baseball players are, I think any of us would have been afraid to change seats at that point. Schiraldi was pulled with runners at first and third. They brought in Bob Stanley, who had thrown just one wild pitch all year, and he almost hit Mookie Wilson in the foot. The ball got away from catcher Rich Gedman. Mitchell scored to tie it 5-5 and Knight moved to second.

We knew right then the game was ours. I just did not expect it to happen on that little dribbler Mookie Wilson hit to first base. Somehow, it got through Bill Buckner's legs and, in a span of ten minutes, we went from complete despair to mobbing Knight at home plate.

After the game, I had to hold my emotions in check because Rhonda Schiraldi, Calvin's sister, came by to see me when it was over. I had met Rhonda at Calvin's wedding the year before. It was just such a weird feeling talking to her after her brother had just been a deciding factor in the Mets' comeback that night. She was obviously upset for him and I could certainly understand because Calvin and I were really good friends. But, hey, I wanted a World Series ring, too!

Since we had done nothing easy in this entire post-season, why should game seven of the World Series be any different? True to form, we fell behind 3-0 and Hurst was throwing a one-hit shutout through five innings.

I thought if we could just get into the Red Sox bullpen, we would really be in great shape. We finally got to Hurst for three runs in the sixth to tie it. When they brought Schiraldi in to start the next inning, I had a feeling the move would backfire.

From what I knew of Calvin and having caught him the previous two years in the minors, I just didn't think it was in his makeup to be a reliever, though he did a good job in that role for Boston. I also knew that he got bothered very easily when things were not going right. In a relief situation, things usually aren't going very well.

We had all the momentum and Calvin had to pitch with the mental burden of knowing he was one out away from winning it two nights ago. It was just a real tough situation for him to be in.

The fans at Shea were chanting "Cal—-vin! Cal—-vin!" the same way the Boston fans rode Darryl Strawberry. It got a lot tougher for Calvin when Knight, the first batter, homered to left center to put us on top. That started a three-run rally.

Boston threw a scare into us in the eighth with two runs, but Jesse Orosco came on and pitched two perfect innings to nail down an 8-5 victory.

It was party time!

I felt a little bit like a fifth wheel in the celebration afterwards because I did not get to play in any of the games. The most exciting part came when I met Mom and Dad in the runway underneath the stands.

The first thing I did was douse them with a big bottle of

champagne. I happened to have a beer in my back pocket and I remembered that I had coaxed Mom into promising that she would drink a beer if we won the World Series.

Now anybody who knows Mom is well aware of her stance on alcohol. Both my parents are very anti-alcohol. We never kept it in our house and even after I turned eighteen, I was forbidden to ever have it on the premises.

Well, I took that beer and almost literally forced Mom to drink it. She drank maybe one-third of it and either spilled or slobbered the rest all over her.

Now Mom would never admit she enjoyed that beer, but I know she enjoyed the moment. It was the best part of the World Series celebration.

A couple hours after the game, it was all Tricia and I could do just to get out of the parking lot. I let Tricia drive my old, green '78 Bonneville because I had partaken of some champagne. Once our car left the secured gate area, the fans were so excited they started climbing onto the hood. Some were taking flash pictures.

I told Tricia to just go ahead and drive. She said: "How can I drive? I can't even see with all these people on the hood." After about ten minutes, we finally got on the road. I wasn't in the mood to do any more celebrating.

That night, most of the team celebrated at Finn McCool's, a Long Island restaurant-bar that was one of the Mets' big hangouts. The owner closed off a section of the restaurant just for the players. I didn't go because I just wanted to find a quiet place to eat and relax. Tricia and I went to an all-night diner in Port Washington, just up the road from my apartment.

I knew if I went to Finn McCool's, it would be one of those all-night affairs where you don't get home until after the sun rises. I wanted to be somewhat alert for the ticker-tape parade that was scheduled for eleven o'clock the next morning. Most of the guys were in rough shape for that. Just about everybody had dark sunglasses on.

I've never seen anything like the confetti shower that greeted us in lower Manhattan. Just the bus ride over to the parade, with all the police escorts, was like being part of a presidential motorcade.

That was probably the most emotional time for me. I thought about all those times in the minors when I almost quit. I had tears in my eyes.

The parade was a bit scary. I was riding in a car with pitcher Sid Fernandez and people were pushing through barricades to get to the cars. The ticker-tape was piled up high all over the place. You could look up and almost get your eyes cut on the stuff as it was falling down.

I wore a sweater that day and the left arm of that sweater was stretched out probably two or three times its size just from people pulling on it. The mayor, Ed Koch, had given us all "I Love N.Y." scarfs, but that was stolen off my neck earlier in the parade. Fans were going nuts.

I was on top of the world that day. I'm glad I savored every moment, too, because never again would that '86 season be duplicated. The end of that year was the last time I can remember really being on a good roll.

I stayed behind in New York for two weeks because the Mets had so many requests for player appearances. I made almost $20,000, half of which I put into a fund for my younger brother, Tom, who was in his last year of college and needed money to start pursuing a professional golf career.

Staying there also gave me an opportunity to spend more time with Tricia and get to know her better. At that point, I had not been dating anyone on a steady basis and was uncertain of where our relationship was going.

What I did seem fairly sure of was that my baseball career finally seemed to be taking off. I had proven myself as a starting catcher, if only on a temporary basis with the Mets.

More than anything, I wanted the chance to be a permanent starter. If not in New York, then with anyone who would give me a shot.

I was more marketable after that '86 season than I had ever

been before. I made it to baseball's pinnacle.

But the fall down that mountain was a lot quicker than the climb up.

The Inside Pitch

True Success

*"A person who gets all wrapped up in himself makes
for a very small package."*

What does success mean to you? How do you tell if a man or woman is successful today? Is it the job they have, the car they drive, the house they live in? Or how much wealth, power and prestige they have accumulated?

Because we live in a country of such abundance, especially when compared to the rest of the world, the American dream for many people often revolves around creating a better lifestyle and adding to our possessions. We relate success to having more money, more toys, more stocks, more property, more World Series rings. When this becomes the focus of our existence, we have basically committed ourselves to a race that is impossible to win.

A great American, Benjamin Franklin, once said: "If a man could have half his wishes, he would double his troubles."

Success in the truest sense of the word cannot be defined by anything material. When a wealthy person dies, people are always asking how much money did he leave? Hey, he left it all. There is no U-Haul behind the hearse.

I do not want to sound like accumulating wealth is inherently bad. That is one of many natural results from the innate characteristic of ambition in all of us. But the final totals are inconsequential to true success. What really matters is not so much the amount you have, but how you acquire it, how you use it and to what extent these possessions consume your life.

Someone once asked John Rockefeller how many millions of dollars it took to be happy. He replied: "It's always the next million."

If that is the case for us, then happiness and success will always be elusive because these are not items to be purchased. Money can buy a house, a bed, a companion, a good time. It cannot buy a home, a good night's sleep, friends and memories.

Anyone who measures success on a calculator or cash register misses the mark. The material possessions we leave behind will eventually be used up, perhaps even wasted. But a person who performs good works, who looks to serve others first, who passes on strong, moral values to their children, who leads an exemplary life worthy of imitation—now that is a legacy of success which endures long after we are gone.

Ewing Kauffman, the late owner of the Kansas City Royals, became one of America's wealthiest men after establishing Marion Laboratories, Inc., a pharmaceutical manufacturing firm, in 1950. His company went from gross sales of $36,000 in its first year into a diversified health care company that now surpasses three billion dollars in annual sales.

But what made this entrepreneur a true success? All the money he made? The championships his baseball team won?

I believe Mr. K, as the Royals players called him, was a success story for reasons beyond those things. He left behind something real, something to uplift his fellow man when he created the Kauffman Foundation. Its mission is to teach young entrepreneurs how to be self-sufficient and productive members of their community. It places special emphasis on helping at-risk youth, provided they follow the rules and regulations established by the program. Kauffman insisted that the foundation, with an endowment of more than one billion dollars, be committed to intense program evaluation so that its work would have a definitive and lasting impact.

America needs more people of Kauffman's vision and philosophy. If all we're concerned about is looking out for number one, it won't matter how much money we have. We will be no different from a caged-up hamster running on an exercise wheel and getting nowhere.

Remember the old proverb that says: "If you want to be rich, give. If you want to be poor, grasp."

A good example of this can be seen in how monkeys are captured in South Africa. Biologists tie a string around a tree, which is then attached to a gourd. The gourd has a long, thin neck with a big based bottom. The monkey sneaks over and smells the sugar and rice that is placed inside as bait. He then sticks his hand all the way down the thin opening of the gourd and gets a big fistful of the goodies.

As the monkey tries to bring his hand back out through the skinny opening, he finds his fist is bigger than the opening. He pulls, screams, wiggles and does back flips trying to get loose. The captor walks over and grabs the monkey!

All the monkey had to do was let go of the treat. Selfishly though, he never lets go.

This story sounds a lot like many of the headlines in our newspapers today. Just replace the monkeys with such names as Pete Rose, Ivan Boesky, Michael Milken or Jimmy Swaggert.

Fortunately, all is not lost. There are signs that America's spirit of goodwill, which enabled it to reach such great heights during and after World War II, is returning. It has been estimated that ninety million people now give an average of three hours a week to charity work. More corporations are getting involved in acts of volunteerism in their communities. The concept of giving back, not just taking, has made an impact on many nationally prominent people.

Olympic gold medalist Jackie Joyner-Kersee also created a foundation. Its first project was developing a community center in an East St. Louis, Ill. neighborhood so kids and senior citizens would have a safe and productive place to spend their time. Domino's pizza owner Tom Monaghan cut back on his business in middle age to do missionary work for the church. Peter Lynch walked away from running Fidelity's Magellan fund with the express purpose of devoting more time to his family and charity work.

There is nothing wrong with having fame and fortune, but we cannot equate those things with success. Just take a look at many of the professional athletes and movie stars who seem to have it made, yet often find themselves turning to drugs, alcohol or other dangerous vices in an attempt to find happiness.

I believe the key is balance, an understanding of where our priorities should lie. The money, the cars, the houses, the boats. It's all cosmetic stuff. What counts is your willingness to share, your relationships, your example, your charity, your reputation, your love. Success is not a commodity, it's a feeling of peace of mind.

The closing lines to Ralph Waldo Emerson's poem, *How Do You Measure Success*, read: "To appreciate beauty. To find the best in others. To leave the world a bit better, whether by a healthy child or redeemed social conditions, or a job well done. To know even one other life has breathed because you lived. This is to have succeeded."

What do all those items have in common? None are for sale.

11

Trading Places— A Royal Disaster

One of the things professional baseball players eventually learn, some a lot harder than others, is you are always a phone call away from being part of a business transaction. Whether you've had a Hall of Fame career or are just scrambling to keep your rear end in the major leagues, nobody is indispensable. With a few exceptions here and there, you can be released, traded or demoted at the slightest whim of anyone with enough power in the organization.

There is no recourse, no appeals hearing, no argument. Just when you think you can get comfortable in one setting, you can be shipped out with the morning mail and be gone before you have a chance to say good-bye.

During that off-season after winning the World Series, rumors had been floating around that the Kansas City Royals wanted to make a deal with the Mets to obtain me. But when the winter meetings passed and nothing happened, I put it out of my mind.

Only a week was left in 1987 spring training and, much to my dismay, my job as Gary Carter's backup was not as sewn up as I thought it was. I had my typical ho-hum spring and found myself in a battle with the same guys, Barry Lyons and John Gibbons, as the year before.

Not that this was a bad situation. Even though New York and I did not exactly fit culturally, I wanted to stay with the Mets because I saw the possibility of playing on two or three more championship teams. The downside was Carter might be there for another five years and I would never get a starting job.

Still, that was an acceptable tradeoff for now. I was looking forward to the following year when the Mets were moving their spring training headquarters to Port St. Lucie, right near my

That feeling did not last long. On the night of March 27, my career took one of those turns that put me right back on the same emotional roller coaster I rode through most of the minor leagues.

Tricia and I were having dinner in my apartment in Clearwater, along with Gibbons and his wife, Julie. I did not have many close friends in the big leagues, but John was special. Even though we competed for the same job, he always encouraged me. Just a real, genuine Christian guy.

Anyway, the phone rang as we were eating. It was Joe McIlvaine, the Mets' general manager. He told me I had been traded to Kansas City as part of a six-player deal and that I was the main player the Royals wanted. When I asked him who the Mets got in return, I remembered being irritated that it was a Triple-A pitching prospect. I thought, "Gee, I'm not worth a major leaguer."

How was I supposed to know that David Cone would go on to become a superstar and make the Mets look like genius wheeler-dealers?

I hung up the phone and told John and his wife: "Well, you've got my job, you might as well have everything in my refrigerator. Take my position, take my groceries. Anything else I can get for you, John?" We had a good laugh.

Not much either of us could smile about after that. John ended up losing the backup job to Barry Lyons and never made it back to the big leagues.

Me? It seemed like old times again. Different team, same knockdown pitch.

A million thoughts were racing through my mind when I drove over to Tampa a couple of days later to meet the Royals, who were supposed to play the Cincinnati Reds in an exhibition game. The team's general manager, John Schuerholz, now with the Atlanta Braves, told me I was going to start the season as a backup to Jim Sundberg, known more for his defense than his bat.

The Royals' plan was for me to gradually move into the starting position later that season. Well, in baseball, things don't always go according to plan.

That game with Cincinnati was rained out and manager Billy Gardner announced there would be a workout back in Fort Myers. I asked him if I could skip it and go back to get the rest of my things from the apartment. He said that was fine.

Five minutes later, Gardner called me back for a private conference to tell me that Sundberg had been traded to the Chicago Cubs and that I was now the starting catcher. Wow! Forty-eight hours ago, I wasn't even sure if I would win the number two job with the 1986 World Series Champions. Now I'm the number one catcher for the 1985 World Series Champions.

Baseball is a funny game. Stick around long enough and you will see just about everything.

Trading Sundberg accelerated things drastically. Now the Royals wanted me at that intra-squad workout because Opening Day was less than a week off and I had not caught any of their pitchers. I can only wonder how differently things might have turned out had Kansas City stuck to its original plan of breaking me in slowly.

At that point, my shoulder had been feeling a little tired and sore, but that dead-arm syndrome was typical for me during springtime. I often had tenderness at the beginning of the year, but it wasn't any big deal to me. I never told the trainers in New York. I never got a rubdown or anything. It was nothing.

No matter what was said then or has been speculated since Cone became a star, I was not damaged goods when I left New York. My arm was fine. It just wasn't very lively in the spring, which is common for many players at that time of year.

When I got to that workout, naturally, I was feeling pumped up and quite eager to impress my new teammates. So I proceeded to throw the ball around a lot harder than I normally would in the spring. Doing that, plus catching every day for the next few days, just made my arm sorer and sorer. I was playing with an arm that was not one-hundred percent, yet with the adrenaline flowing, I really aired it out. I believe that's when I became susceptible to injury.

By the time we broke camp, my arm was hurting so badly that I told them I needed a day off from that last exhibition game with the Memphis Chicks, our minor league club. No way was I going to sit out the opening game the next afternoon against the Chicago White Sox, so I loaded up on Tylenol and aspirin to deaden the pain.

Unfortunately, this was no minor blemish. Some things just aren't very easy to cover up.

It's hard for players to stay excited through a 162-game season, but Opening Day is never a problem, especially in a baseball-minded town like Kansas City.

On April 6, 1987, I was as excited as I've ever been taking the field. It was my first day as a big-league starting catcher. I was twenty-six years old and finally had achieved what I had been working for all my life.

But I also felt more apprehension than in all my previous Major League games. Many factors wore heavily on my mind.

The time crunch of arriving so late in spring training allowed me only one opportunity to catch each of the Royals' starting pitchers before Opening Day. Two of the biggest catching challenges were Danny Jackson and Mark Gubicza. They were two of our hardest throwers and their pitches moved an awful lot. I had to catch Jackson in my first game in Royals Stadium.

Fortunately, the White Sox were not much of a base-stealing team and I got through that first series without looking too bad. I had four hits in six at-bats and had the game-winning RBI in my second game. But my arm felt lousy, which was something I could no longer hide from the coaches even if I wanted to.

I did not catch for the next four games, which obviously raised the curiosity of the Kansas City media. The team attributed it to a virus to protect me.

But after two home games against the Detroit Tigers and an April 18 game at Yankee Stadium, it became apparent that my arm was only getting worse and a decision needed to be made. Designated hitter George Orta was coming off the disabled list. To make room for him, either catcher Larry Owen or Jamie Quirk had to be sent to Triple-A or I had to go on the fourteen-day DL.

It was a no-brainer. The club would rather have me miss some games now than a lot more later on, so they flew me back to Kansas City for X-rays to make sure nothing was seriously wrong.

Given my medical history, I had every reason to be nervous.

Dr. Steve Joyce, the Royals' team physician, did an arthrogram at St. Luke's Hospital and it revealed a small tear in the rotator cuff muscle. Rest was prescribed for the remainder of the two-week period, but when the pain didn't go away, my disability time was extended to four weeks, then six weeks.

Finally, the club decided I should go to Los Angeles and let the country's premiere sports surgeon, Dr. Frank Jobe, look me over. After he manipulated my shoulder, he confirmed the tear, but also believed there was damage to the anterior portion of the shoulder. That's the front part where the ligaments are.

He recommended arthroscopic surgery. Jobe also said there was a very good chance that he would have to open up my shoulder and do a total reconstructive procedure on my throwing arm. So much for playing baseball in 1987.

On June 30, Jobe performed surgery on me that had never been attempted before on a major league ballplayer. It was done successfully on Chicago Bears quarterback Jim McMahon, though it took him quite a while to return to full speed. They could not tell me for certain when I would fully recover, but the hope was I could return for 1988 spring training.

I'm glad I never knew then what wishful thinking that was or it would have made all those days in rehabilitation seem so much longer.

The problem was, the catching position is so much different than any others because you're always having to make quick, off-balance throws. It's probably worse for catchers than pitchers to come back from this type of surgery because pitchers usually have good balance when they throw and that really reduces the stress on the arm.

Mentally, this was a devastating setback. I was just breaking in with a new team, and now I didn't even feel a part of the Royals. My shoulder was put into a sling and elevated by a foam lunch bucket for two weeks.

By the middle of that '87 season, it was a major feat just to throw the ball ten feet with no pain.

I couldn't even scratch my back with my right hand. When you have rotator cuff surgery, so many things you never give a second thought to can mess up the rehabilitation. You might suddenly slap at an insect bite or jerk your arm away from a flare-up on the barbeque grill.

You have to be so careful. Any sudden motion of the arm can set you back weeks or months.

If it hadn't been for Tricia, who was still working as a nurse in New York, I would have died from boredom that season. No matter how much encouragement you get from teammates, coaches and trainers, a player does not feel like a player when he comes to the park every day just to exercise and rehabilitate.

This time, getting hurt did have an up side. It gave me an opportunity to spend more time developing my relationship with Tricia. I had started to get a special feeling about her. There was something about Tricia that just seemed so right.

You know how you connect with someone for no one specific reason? It's like trying to explain why you like the feel of a certain shoe. You can't. All you know is that it fits.

In late July, I flew out to Los Angeles for a checkup with Dr. Jobe and he reassured me that he thought I would be able to come back and play sometime in '88. By that time, I made up my mind to ask Tricia to marry me, so I called her parents from Dr. Jobe's office to get their permission.

I'm rather old-fashioned about that stuff and I also knew Tricia's parents would appreciate it. Well, when I phoned them to ask for her hand in marriage, there was a long silence.

Uh, oh! Was it something I said? Luckily, the pause was not because they questioned me marrying their daughter. I just caught them off guard. When they finally got some words out, they were excited. But I told them to keep it a secret because I had a neat and daring proposal in mind.

The first weekend in August was Tricia's birthday and one thing she said she always wanted to do was go on a hot-air balloon ride. I was scared to death of heights. The idea did not overly thrill me, but I knew she would enjoy it. So I made arrangements with this guy to go up in a balloon at Richards-Gebaur Air Force base, just south of Kansas City.

All I told Tricia was that her birthday present was contingent upon good weather. When we got to the open field and she saw the balloons, Tricia was very excited.

Little did she know that was just the appetizer.

There were two other patrons in other balloons near us ready to go up at the same time. What Tricia was unaware of was I had already made a banner out of a white bed sheet and put two wooden broom handles on each end. I painted on it: "Will You Marry Me, Sweet Pea?" with a heart next to it.

Sweet Pea was my nickname for Tricia. When she wasn't looking, I gave the banner to the pilot of another balloon and told him to unroll it in mid-flight and hang it on the side of the balloon.

About eight-hundred feet up and fifty yards from the other balloon, the pilot began to unveil the banner before we got separated too much. Tricia did not see it. Finally, our captain says: "Hey, look over there."

When Tricia saw that proposal banner, she just broke into tears. Then I pulled the engagement ring out of my pocket. I decided not to put it on her hand because she was shaking so badly. I was afraid she would drop it overboard.

So I kept the ring in my pocket. We had some champagne in flight and toasted our future together. It was very emotional for both of us.

On that August night, I conquered two of my biggest fears—heights and marriage!

Making wedding plans was fun. It provided a nice diversion

from the mental drudgery of constantly rehabilitating my shoulder. Besides Tricia, a major factor in getting through that '87 season was the attitude the Royals showed toward me.

They did not just ignore me because I was on the DL. John Schuerholz and John Wathan, who took over as manager for Billy Gardner, did not try to push me to come back before I was ready.

The longer that year wore on, the more the timetable for my return kept getting pushed back. First, it was spring training of 1988, then May of that year, then June. . . . July. . . . August.

Pretty soon, I started to wonder if I would ever come back. Even when that time came, I would always have that rotator cuff stigma following me around everywhere I went.

But one thing, above all else, kept me going. I did not want to be watching a ballgame on television when I was forty-five years old and be a bitter man. I had already battled through baseball hardships that many guys would have never made it through.

You have to find ways to stay motivated because rehab wears you down mentally. I kept an article from a Kansas City paper taped to my mirror that summer which said I would never catch again. It was just something to motivate me. When you are out of the game and uncertain if you will ever come back, every day is a battle to tune out the negative.

I often wondered when riding a stationary bike or doing boring range-of-motion exercises about all those bonus babies who had it easy. I would think: "How come it hasn't been that easy for me?"

The Royals finished just two games behind the Minnesota Twins in the American League West race in 1987. The Twins went on to win the World Series. I could not help thinking how I might have been able to change that outcome if I had only been healthy.

It's only human to have those thoughts, but you cannot let them consume you. Coming back from injuries is hard enough. Pour self-pity on top of it and you have yourself a much tougher ballgame.

When my baseball career was over, I wanted to know inside that I had done everything humanly possible to succeed. If that wasn't enough, then I could at least move on without lugging a heavy bag of regret everywhere.

I did not catch one pitch from April 19, 1987, to August 12, 1988. In-between, Tricia and I got married. Every day, I thank God for that catch.

Our wedding in Fort Pierce was probably the most fun I have ever had in my life. With Calvin Schiraldi serving as one of my groomsmen, I also knew there was going to be some fun at my expense.

Calvin owed me big-time from all the stuff I pulled at his wedding two years earlier in Jackson, Miss. I did not know how or when, but I knew pay-back time was coming.

At the rehearsal dinner the night before the wedding, I gave all my groomsmen radio headsets for gifts, but got something different for Calvin. I gave Mr. Red Sox relief ace a framed picture of our 1986 Mets World Series team.

The minute I did that, he tapped his glass to get everyone's attention and proceeded to tell them how I sabotaged his wedding. Then he reached down into a duffel bag and pulled out these T-shirts with my picture on it.

It was a photo he took of me when we were roommates in Triple-A ball in Tidewater. I had just gotten up from a nap and walked over to the kitchen in my birthday suit. Calvin snapped a picture of me in the buff from the back side. He said long ago that he would get me with it some day. That day was here.

Calvin had that picture screened on to those T-shirts with the caption: "Ed Hearn Fanny Club." He presented one to everybody at the rehearsal dinner.

At the wedding reception the next day, that same photo was on everyone's table at the Monte Carlo Country Club. The minister who married us, Rev. Tim Robertson, enjoyed the gag as much as anyone. He was the baseball chaplain for the Jackson Mets when Calvin and I played there in 1984.

Just to make sure Calvin's revenge was thorough and complete, he paid off the limousine driver to get into my suitcases. He filled them with rice and assorted items. I suppose I should be grateful he didn't pack some Limburger cheese along with it.

Our honeymoon was not only romantic, it was the perfect getaway from baseball, from rehabilitation, from all the uncertainty about when I would play again.

We went to Peter Island in the British Virgin Islands, a quiet place owned by the Amway Corporation. It only had accommodations for maybe thirty couples. Nobody lived on the island. Even the employees were boated in every morning from one of the main islands.

You could go snorkeling, sailing, horseback riding or take a little tour bus to other private beaches around the island. It was so secluded, you could go almost an entire day without seeing anyone.

But I could not put baseball totally out of my mind. I brought my dumbbells, glove and ball and continued my rehab. Tricia and I actually played long-toss together on the beach so my arm would continue to get stronger.

I almost wish we could have stayed on that island for the rest of my rehabilitation. Working out and not playing real baseball did not seem so bad when we were in paradise.

Doing it every day at Royals Stadium was just a constant reminder of what I was missing.

It took almost nine seasons to get to the big leagues with the New York Mets. But the time it took to get back into a Kansas City Royals uniform felt like an eternity.

The Inside Pitch

Playing the Hand You're Dealt

"There's no education like adversity."

In 1987, I experienced the first major setback of my life—a potential career-ending shoulder injury. For the next three years, it was a battle to regain my stature as a healthy major league ballplayer, as well as deal with all the negative press and fan reaction around Kansas City involving "the trade."

Fans would call in on talk-radio shows and absolutely bury me. It was almost as if they thought I wanted to get hurt, wanted to miss out on the opportunity to establish myself as a big-league catcher, wanted to miss out on making the millions of dollars that lay in store for me.

It was a gut-wrenching time. The pain in my shoulder almost paled in comparison to the day-to-day agony of being made to feel that I let everybody down. It just didn't seem fair.

Tom Landry, the former Dallas Cowboys coach, once said: "The most important thing about adversity is that it will bring out the best or worst in all of us."

How right he is. The reality is that all of us are going to face some tremendous challenges at some point in life. That's part of the journey. None of us are immune to it. Remember the cute line that reminds us: "The only one with his problems behind him is the school bus driver."

The question is not whether you will have adversity. It's a matter of when. So, the key is learning how to deal with it. As Mike Murdock says: "Winners are not people without any problems. Winners are people who have learned how to overcome their problems."

I have come to believe that adversity, in and of itself, is not all bad. Adversity is the training ground upon which all great men and women develop the character to go on to have a major impact on society. But it often takes overcoming setbacks that seem insurmountable.

Many years ago, a young Midwestern lawyer suffered such deep depression that his friends thought it best to keep all knives and razors away from him. During this time, he wrote: "I am now the most miserable man living. Whether I shall ever be better, I cannot tell. I'm awfully forebode I shall not recover." As it turned out, he was wrong. He did recover, and went on to become one of America's most beloved presidents—Abraham Lincoln.

One of my former teammates with the Royals, outfielder Jim Eisenreich, spent the early part of his career with the Minnesota Twins. He played 34 games for Minnesota before being placed on the disabled list with a neurological disorder. It was later diagnosed as Tourette Syndrome, which causes the body to twitch nervously. It can be controlled with medication, but one thing Eisenreich could not control was the cruel manner that fans sometimes treated him when he went on the road.

They made fun of his condition, which later resurfaced to the point where Eisenreich retired in 1984. He went home to St. Cloud, Minn. and everyone figured he was done with baseball. The Royals discovered him playing amateur ball and signed him after the '86 season.

From there, Eisenreich authored one of baseball's greatest comeback stories. He ended up playing all or parts of five seasons with Kansas City before signing with the Philadelphia Phillies in 1993. Eisenreich's condition was still there, but so was his determination to battle through it.

In that '93 season, he batted .318 with seven home runs and fifty-four RBI's. He was an unsung hero as Philadelphia captured the National League pennant. Adversity brought out the best in Jim Eisenreich. He was thought to be finished at age twenty-five. Last year, he was still in the big leagues with the Phillies at age thirty-six.

Thomas Payne talks about adversity's role in our lives when he says: "The harder the conflict, the more glorious the triumph. What we attain too cheap, we esteem too lightly. I love that man that can smile in trouble, that can gather strength from distress and grow brave by reflection."

One such man is Dick Hathaway, a good friend of mine and world renowned body-builder. His story, about one of life's most devastating challenges, is both gripping and courageous.

In October 1992, Dick was preparing to recapture the "Natural Mr. Universe" title. He had been hosting his own syndicated national television exercise and nutrition show. Then, in an ironic twist of fate, this picture of health was stricken with leukemia. He was told that even if a perfect bone marrow donor was found, his chance of survival was only fifty-fifty.

Shortly thereafter, his prayers were answered. His only sibling, a brother, was found to be a perfect match. He then immediately began extensive doses of chemotherapy, full body radiation and a bone marrow transplant.

But, after being released from the hospital, he found he had lost fifty pounds of precious muscle mass. Despite his condition, he was determined not only to survive, but to again return to the peak condition he was in prior to the leukemia.

Even though he had no hair or fingernails, had to wear a mask, and could barely lift a ten-pound dumbbell, Dick returned to the gym and began his comeback. He realized that a journey of a thousand miles begins with a single step.

Through incredible dedication and perseverance, Dick regained his fifty pounds and returned to competition. Less than two years removed from transplant surgery, he recaptured the Natural Mr. Universe title.

Today, Dick shares his inspiring story not only with other leukemia patients, but others around the country as a motivational speaker. He has turned an obstacle into an opportunity, a stumbling block into a stepping stone.

Sometimes, the hardest thing to realize when adversity hits us is God often wants to allow a greater victory to occur. He seems to delight in taking someone's mess and working a miracle.

Adversity forces us to evaluate what we believe, what our goals are, and the methods we have been using to achieve our goals. Almost every achiever has faced adversity that unlocked the doors to his greatest accomplishments.

Winston Churchill, one of the greatest speakers of our time, stuttered as a child. Beethoven wrote some of his best music after he went totally deaf.

No matter what obstacles lay before us, we have a choice. Either let them defeat us or seize the opportunity.

12

Take Me Out
of the Ball Game

*F*inally, in the baseball dog days of August, I saw a glimmer of hope. The Kansas City Royals were pretty much out of the 1988 pennant race, but my race to re-establish myself as a major league catcher was just getting started.

The Royals sent me to their Class A team in Baseball City, Fla. to get my first taste of game experience after a sixteen-month lay-off. My arm was pain-free and in my rehabilitation program, I was throwing balls up to 180 feet, thirty times a day. I just needed to get the rust off after not playing for so long.

I passed the three-week trial in the minors, hitting .304 in seventeen games before the Royals called me back up on September 2nd. Five days later, I felt like a kid again. I was back behind the plate at Royals Stadium against the California Angels, wondering if that Kansas City columnist who wrote that I would never catch again was sitting up in the press box. If I had known for sure, I would have paid a delivery boy to serve him a knife, fork, plate and a healthy helping of crow.

The media is entitled to their opinion. I'm professional enough to take criticism without complaining when it's warranted. But when somebody who is not in the medical field wrote that I would never catch again, and just contradicted the opinion of someone like Dr. Frank Jobe without any attempt to get the facts, that really chafed me. Basically, that columnist was saying I did not have what it took to make a comeback from rotator cuff surgery.

My arm and body might have built up some rust, but as long as my willingness to compete was there, nothing or nobody was going to convince me that I could not play the game of baseball.

In my first at-bat, facing Chuck Finley, I doubled to left field off the glove of Mike Brown. It wasn't as impressive as Bo

Jackson's two-run triple the inning before or George Brett's home run the inning after, but it sure beat making a living by writing bone-headed conjecture.

What hurt as much as anything during my long layoff was knowing the Royals could never escape the shadow of David Cone. It was like this ghost hovering over the front-office. You could never read or hear my name without Cone coming up.

I'm sure it didn't help matters that Cone grew up in the Kansas City area. But sometimes baseball is a roll of the dice. Nobody can predict when or if injuries are going to strike.

What people often forget is that Cone had arm problems for a good part of that 1987 season and was forced to sit out. He could just as easily have been a regular customer of Dr. Jobe. Fortunately, his ailments were not as severe as mine and he was able to recover in a couple of months.

But how in the world was John Schuerholz, a guy now considered one of baseball's top executives, supposed to know whose career would go into limbo? He can judge talent, but he's not psychic.

The Royals needed a front-line catcher and one of their top scouts, Tom Ferrick, urged Schuerholz to make the deal for me based on what he saw when I took over for Gary Carter during the 1986 season. I was perfectly healthy then. To this day, I still believe if I had not overextended myself those first two weeks I was with the Royals, my baseball career would be remembered for other things than being an answer to a trivia question on the David Cone trade.

Deep down, I knew the Royals believed that too, but it became apparent during that '88 season that having Cone thrown in their face all the time was baggage they were tired of carrying.

At the winter baseball meetings that year, Schuerholz was quoted by the Associated Press as saying: "Even my eight-year-old son knows the worst deal I ever made. He asks me, 'Daddy, why did you trade David Cone?' "

I guess Schuerholz's son forgot about that game-winning, pinch-hit single I delivered in the tenth inning against the

Chicago White Sox on September 29th of that season. Or the two doubles I had the following day (my last major league hits, as it turned out).

I mean, what did Cone do? Except win twenty games for the first-place Mets that season, finish with the second-best ERA in the National League (2.22), win 104 games over the next seven years and twice lead the NL in strikeouts.

Seriously, I'm indebted to David Cone. He's a good guy and I'm glad for all his success. If nothing else, that trade has been a great ice-breaker with audiences in my speaking career.

Keep it up, Dave, but don't expect any royalties. Not with that Brinks truck you use to cash your monthly paychecks.

The beginning of the end of my baseball career came during the 1989 season, which has to go down as the most exasperating time I ever spent in the minors. I had my share of frustrations to that point, but that season with the Triple-A Omaha Royals was enough to ruin any player's love for the game.

It wasn't anything the Royals' organization did to me as much as the free rein they apparently gave to Sal Rende, the Omaha manager. In my thirteen years of professional ball, Rende was the only manager that I could not get along with.

I really did not mind being sent to Omaha. The Royals had signed forty-one-year-old Bob Boone in the off-season because both Mike Macfarlane and I had question marks hanging over us.

Mike had been demoted to Triple-A the previous year because the Royals wanted him to improve his catching skills. I was still trying to prove my throwing arm was of big-league quality. Since I could get more playing time in Omaha, the Royals gave Mike the backup catching job in the spring, which I understood perfectly.

The whole idea behind me going to Triple-A was to catch as often as possible. That's what the Royals told me coming out of spring training. Those were the marching orders given to Rende, but it was not long before I found myself sitting more on the bench than squatting behind home plate.

Instead of playing on a regular basis, Sal had me splitting time with Kevin Burrell, who had been with him the year before at Double-A Memphis. If Burrell was a hot-shot prospect or was having a great season, I could see it. But he barely hit his weight (.217 batting average) and was very suspect defensively, though he had a cannon-like arm.

Sal and I just had a rocky relationship, partly because I wasn't the type of player who ever kissed up to anybody. I know there are people who play that game as a matter of survival, but I absolutely refuse to do it. Judge me by my ability to perform a job, not by my willingness to massage the boss's ego.

For whatever reason, Sal carried a big chip on his shoulder everywhere he went, particularly toward players that had already been in the big leagues. It was almost as if he was jealous of them. Sal spent seven years as a minor leaguer in the Cleveland Indians' farm system, but never got to The Show.

His teams have done well over the years. Sal managed Omaha for two more years after I was gone. He was picked by *The Sporting News* as Minor League Manager of the Year in 1990. But I guarantee you he would not have gotten my vote or the vote of most of the players on our team.

Within a month of getting to Omaha, Sal basically buried me for absolutely no just cause. Instead of being the team's primary catcher, it reached the point where I was lucky if I caught one out of three games.

Pitchers like Kevin Appier, Ed Olwine and Steve Crawford were always asking me: "Why aren't you catching tonight?" The truth is, they wanted to throw to me, but there was nothing I could do about it.

Sal Rende saw to it that I would not get back to the big leagues and I guess he did it by turning in unfavorable reports to Kansas City about me. There is no way the Royals would have soured on me that season without Rende doing that.

I got so disgusted about my lack of playing time that I called the Royals' minor league director, John Boles, who happens to be buddy-buddy with Sal (both of them are now in the Florida

Marlins system), and got the typical run-around. He said Sal was running the team and it was up to him.

It just didn't add up. Coming out of spring, the Royals wanted me to play so I could develop and get back to Kansas City as quickly as possible. Now I was a bench warmer hitting .281 and going nowhere.

At that point, it became obvious the Royals were starting to give up on me. Or advised to give up on me.

Here's the irony of the whole deal. I was good enough to be named to the Triple-A All Star team, but not good enough to start on my own team.

I hurt my knee after the All Star break, which also cut into my playing time, but by then my role had already been carved in stone. Sal Rende saw to it that I would be nothing more than yesterday's news.

One thing I never wanted when I left baseball was to harbor any bitterness about anything, but to this day, I still have bitter feelings about the way I was handled in Omaha.

Sal Rende succeeded in tearing me down mentally and emotionally. I've handled my share of adversity in baseball, as have many other players for different reasons, but what I went through in Omaha really caused me to sour on baseball for the first time in my life.

If I wasn't good enough, fine. Just shoot straight with me. I hold no resentment for not making it back to Kansas City. What I resented was not being given the chance to prove myself when that was supposed to be the plan coming out of spring training.

Maybe I wasn't seeing the whole situation clearly. Maybe I was letting pride cloud my judgment.

But there is no maybe about this: after one season with my pal Sal, the fun of playing baseball was going, going, . . . gone.

Going into 1990 spring training, I had strong vibrations that my days with the Royals were numbered. I had no leverage to get any better deals elsewhere, so I went back to camp as a non-roster player.

Initially, things worked out fine. I was catching as well as any-body and throwing out runners better than ever in springtime. My arm felt good, but the club had only two or three weeks to evalu-ate me because of the player lockout in March.

There was never a question that I could swing the bat. I felt like I showed improvement defensively. The manager, John Wathan, and several of the coaches told me they were amazed at how well I progressed. Or maybe they were using those reports on me from the previous season as a barometer. I'm not sure.

But the Royals didn't get much time to give me a proper look that spring and decisions had to be made. So on April 3—three years and a week after they gave up David Cone to get me—I was history. They gave me my release.

I think the Royals, particularly Schuerholz, just reached the point where they did not want the constant reminder of the Cone trade hovering over them any more. They wanted to put it behind them, start fresh. I honestly don't blame them for that.

Kansas City offered me a job as a minor league instructor, but I felt I could still play and wanted to pursue other opportunities.

As an overall organization, the Royals were great to me. They were more patient than a lot of big-league clubs would have been in my injury situation. My feelings toward Rende in no way changes what I think about Kansas City. It's a class organization and a superb city. I would not make it my home if I thought oth-erwise.

I just wish I could have paid back the faith the Royals showed in me with a greater contribution on the field. I'm sorry John Schuerholz had to take as much abuse as he did for making that trade. That was never right or fair.

But a lot of things about baseball are not right or fair. Life is the same way. You just deal with it and, hopefully, move on.

After six weeks on the unemployment line, the Cleveland Indians signed me and shipped me to their Double-A club in Canton, Ohio. All with the understanding that when I got myself back into playing shape and proved I was ready to go, they were going to move me out of Canton. Supposedly, once I was ready, they were going to trade big league back-up catcher Joel Skinner to Houston and I would be called up to back-up Sandy Alomar. At the very least, they said I would be moved up to Triple-A in a couple of weeks.

I went to Canton with a great attitude and immediately showed the lay off hadn't hampered me at all. After just ten days there, I was hitting .500, with two home runs, nine RBI's and was throwing the ball well. But, days turned into weeks, and weeks into months. Nothing was happening on the trade front and I was getting pretty fed up. I eventually began to get real frustrated with the organization for not following through on their word. I certainly had held up my end of the bargain.

As time wore on, my hitting cooled off—finishing with a .270 average in twenty-nine games. The one salvation for me in Canton was I really enjoyed playing for their manager, Ken Bolek. He seemed to appreciate that I worked with their young pitching staff and nurtured them along, particularly Charles Nagy, who was really just learning how to pitch at that time.

Being twenty-nine years old and working with all these kids, I felt like the Crash Davis character in the movie *Bull Durham*. At my age, that's not where I wanted to be and Bolek sympathized with my frustration.

Unfortunately, there was not much he could do about it. So I finally decided to make the break after an episode that can only be described as "The Bus Ride From Hell."

We were on our way home from a road trip to London, Ontario (Canada), which is 319 miles from Canton. We left at six o'clock at night, which should put us in our beds around midnight.

First, the bus overheated and the air conditioner broke, so we sat alongside the road for an hour waiting on repairs. Then one of our players, Francisco Melendez, hit his head on a latch as he tried to close a window and blood started gushing out of him. We had to take him to a hospital to get stitches and ended up waiting two hours.

On the road, the bus broke down again. Another two-hour wait for a new bus. Then you add transferring all the equipment and luggage for twenty-seven people.

A six-hour bus ride turned into an eleven hour nightmare. We got home a little after five in the morning.

I got off that bus and said: "That's it. I'll never ride another minor league bus again." I told Tricia that I would finish out the last homestand before the All Star break, but after that, we were going back to Kansas City and starting life over.

If I couldn't be in the big leagues, or at least Triple-A, then it was time to say good-bye. I was turning thirty in another month and I had better things to do than riding buses in Double-A and playing guidance counselor.

See ya. I packed my bags and drove back to Kansas City.

This was really it. No turning back. But when I got home, there was a message on my phone that the Indians had traded away a Triple-A catcher and would I report to their Colorado Springs team in the Pacific Coast League.

At that point, I could not have been more down on baseball. Tricia and I faced a major decision. I really was not up for giving this another shot, but one thing that really intrigued me was I love Colorado. It was only a half-season, so I gave it a whirl.

I did not regret it. In fact, though I played only five weeks there, it was a great time. We had some talented players (Carlos Baerga, Turner Ward, Stan Jefferson, Beau Allred, Alan Cockrell, to name a few) and I got to play for maybe the best manager I ever had in my entire career, Charlie Manuel. He is now the Cleveland Indians' hitting coach.

I split time with another catcher, Tom Magrann, and played very well. In seventeen games, I hit .288 with eight RBI's and felt almost certain that I would get called up to Cleveland when the rosters expanded in September.

But, as luck would have it, we were playing a home game in mid-August and one of the fastest guys in the league tried to steal on me. The pitch was low and away and I had to sidearm a throw to second base. When I put a little extra on the throw, I felt my shoulder twinge and thought I really hurt it badly.

That won me another expense-paid trip to Los Angeles to see Dr. Jobe. He told me I just strained the shoulder and no surgery was necessary. I would be fine by spring training.

Cleveland felt like I showed everyone I could play and that if my arm was sound in the spring, they said they wanted me back. I think they were just feeding me a line. I worked hard over the winter with my cousin Jeff Datz—a catcher who reached the big leagues briefly with the Detroit Tigers—to get ready for the 1991 season. But I heard nothing from Cleveland.

No surprise, really. The Indians were young and building. They did not need a thirty-year-old-catcher with a suspect arm. Neither did anybody else.

What few offers I had were jobs in the lower minors. Thanks, but I had been there and done that too many times. In the spring of '91, I said good-bye to baseball for good. I didn't even want to be in the country on Opening Day, so Tricia and I took a cruise to the Western Caribbean.

Better to be riding on a love boat than on some stinkin' bus heading for another Double-A armpit.

So now what was I supposed to do with the rest of my life? I had gotten some career counseling over the winter at a local junior college, which led to some interview opportunities in the insurance business.

When we got home from the cruise, I went through a bunch of interviews with different people and ended up taking a job with New York Life, which is still the company I'm with today.

I started with them in June of '91. In no time at all, I would be in dire need of the very product I was selling. Baseball had thrown me so many curves in thirteen years. I had faced just about every kind of adversity there was.

But nothing like what was about to hit me. Thank God that through it all, I had a wife who stood by me in my darkest hour.

The Inside Pitch

Marriage Vows

"...for better or worse, for richer or poorer, until death do us part."

Statistics tell us that at this time in Western culture, the chances are fifty-fifty that a marriage will lead to divorce. Flip a coin. One of every two marriages will end up on the rocks.

They also say that if one or both partners are still teenagers, the odds for failing become even higher. If either partner has witnessed an unhappy marriage between their parents, the odds increase again. If one or both partners come from broken homes, the odds rise still higher. If there has been regular sexual involvement before marriage, or if either partner abuses alcohol or drugs, the odds skyrocket.

We live in an age where marriage is anything but easy. Too often, the only words that describe many marriages are ones like pain, suffering, destruction, grief, abuse and heartbreak.

Although I may have been unlucky the past eight years in some areas of my life, my marriage to Tricia has been the greatest thing that ever happened to me. As many of you know, finding the right partner can be one of the most fulfilling experiences of a lifetime.

Tricia has been more than just a wife. She is my soul mate, my best friend, my absolute rock when times were tough. Without her love and support, I'd be in a pine box today instead of enjoying life, family and all the blessings that go with it. She has stuck with me through thick and thin, mostly thin.

So many times in today's society, people get involved in marriage for so many of the wrong reasons. In baseball, I saw many marriages fail because it seemed that one or both of the spouses were focused on something else besides love when they went to the altar.

When Tricia and I met, I was reaching the peak of my professional baseball career. It seemed as though I had the world in the palm of my hand. The future looked ever so promising.

At that time, it was so easy to spot the women who were chasing ballplayers because of the wealth and prestige that these guys had as a result of their profession. It's not much different from the gold-diggers who pursue the big game of doctors, lawyers and such.

If Tricia had any thoughts of snagging a wealthy ballplayer, those dreams would have been quickly shattered. To be quite honest, after all the things I began to go through started happening, it would have been so easy for her to jump ship. After all, I was not the cheeriest guy in the world when things fell apart.

True love is not like a retractable pen. As the words to the song go: "When I fall in love, it will be forever."

A man and woman must commit to walk many miles together through what is sometimes a deep, dark forest. But it can be a journey of incredible fulfillment. It is only in the experience of love that a human being can discover the fullness of life that all of us innately desire.

For me, the following excerpts from a poem really bears out the essence of the journey toward true love:

Love seeks to give, lust seeks to get.
Love is the giving of, lust is the striving for.
Love is selfless, lust is selfish.
Love seeks to give and forgive, lust seeks to get then forgets.

Author unknown

I am so thankful every day of my life that Tricia has been there with me through the darkest of times. She has allowed me to experience this fullness of life.

Tricia, I love you. Thanks so much for being "the wind beneath my wings."

13

Donor Means Giving, Not Giving Up

*I*t had been fourteen years since my high school football physical revealed that the creatinine levels in my blood and urine were abnormal. Doctors told me this might be an indication that someday I could encounter problems with my kidneys. I figured what they meant was way down the road. Maybe when I was sixty or seventy-years-old. Not thirty-one!

Each year, just as a precautionary measure, I would get my blood checked to make sure everything was stable. All my years in professional baseball, things were fine.

But when the doctor's office phoned in late July 1991, and asked if Tricia and I could come in to discuss the latest test results, we immediately got the feeling that the news couldn't be good. We were right.

Dr. Jim Mertz, my primary physician, sat us down and one of the first things he said was that he didn't know how I could have played professional baseball for as long as I did. I leaned forward and said: "Doc, I was good." Then he replied: "No, you don't understand."

That's when he informed me that my kidneys were in a declining stage, and that possibly within six or twelve months, I would have to go on dialysis and eventually need a transplant.

When I heard that, you could have hit me over the head with a sledgehammer. I wouldn't have felt a thing. I was that numb. The news just blew me away.

I just lost a baseball career. Now the doctor was telling me my life was in danger, too.

No, this couldn't be happening. Not to me. It's not like I was an old man. I was just moving into my prime. Get out of here with that dialysis and transplant stuff.

I went home that day in denial. No matter how much Tricia

tried to help me stay upbeat, I just couldn't accept that what Dr. Mertz told me was true.

A few weeks later, another phone call. Another medical alert. My Mom said that Tom, my younger brother, had been diagnosed with hypogammaglobulinemia, a condition in which the body doesn't produce enough antibodies to fight off infection.

Since I had the same problem as a child before outgrowing it, she advised that I get tested again. Bang! Come to find out, some of my test results were worse than Tom's.

I was referred to an immunologist, Dr. Nabih Abdou, and he started running a series of tests on my whole family to determine if this was a hereditary problem. Mom was also diagnosed with the condition. It turns out Debbie, being adopted, was the only one whose gamma globulin levels were completely normal.

On August 6, 1991, I began monthly gamma globulin infusion treatments, which cost $2,500 and are something I'll probably have to have the rest of my life unless my body starts producing enough of these immunities.

Well, this was just peachy. Here I was, just getting adjusted to being out of baseball and starting a new career. Now this medical double whammy hit me. Wasn't it bad enough that baseball ended for me just as I was in a position to make great money?

I knew guys retired from the Kansas City Royals that were financially set for the rest of their lives, maybe even their children's lives. They had trouble figuring out what to do to keep from getting bored without baseball, but at least they had the luxury of procrastinating.

Not me. Over thirteen years, counting my World Series bonus, I only made about $300,000. I was in no position to take a couple of years off. I had to hustle and make a conscious effort to get some income going again.

Now I had to do it with two big strikes against me—kidneys that were heading toward renal failure and a suspect immune system which required monthly IV treatments.

So I returned to my insurance business with New York Life

and tried to focus totally on work, but the daily reminders of my deteriorating condition were always there. Tricia went back to work full time as a school nurse to ensure some steady income and most importantly, our health insurance.

My creatinine levels had to be constantly monitored. That was done by urinating into these jugs in twenty-four hour intervals, then having those specimens taken to the lab for testing.

By the end of 1991, I was still in somewhat of a partial denial state. Well, maybe not denial, but I was content to let Tricia handle all the communication with Dr. Mertz about my condition.

Apparently, things were getting worse than I had anticipated at the time. I could feel myself becoming more fatigued and weak around the holidays, but Tricia never went into any great detail about my creatinine levels. Not that I was in any mood to hear about it because there was nothing I could have done to combat the inevitable.

Tricia knew it was getting to the point where dialysis was close to imminent. She just didn't want me worrying about what I couldn't control.

No sense putting a complete damper on Christmas.

I wasn't in much of a celebrating mood on December 25, 1991. The only other Christmas I could remember being this much of a downer was the one I had to spend in Colombia, South America, in winter ball, but at least I was a healthy young man then.

Eight years later, I felt old and dilapidated. I came down the stairs that Christmas, not really in the spirit of things, and headed for the kitchen to get something to eat. Tricia said: "Oh, look what Santa brought us."

She pulled me into the living room where our tree was and the first thing I noticed was this box that contained a shipment of drugs for my monthly IV transfusion. "Oh, great. Santa brought me some more medicine," I said.

Then, out of the corner of my eye, I saw something black in one of the stockings and it moved. I looked closer and it was a little Black Labrador puppy. I was really surprised because Tricia and I never talked about getting a dog, but I think she knew that I was going to need a little something to keep me going.

Seeing that puppy, I was almost in shock. It brought tears to my eyes. I had always wanted a hunting/outdoor dog, but we just never felt the time was right to have a dog. Hunting had become a new love for me because there weren't as many good fishing places in Kansas City as there were back home in Florida.

The puppy was only a few weeks old and looked so cute in that stocking. It just made a tough Christmas a lot brighter. Appropriately, I named him Hunter.

Tricia knew I always loved dogs, particularly this kind of dog. The great thing about a dog is you can tell him all your problems and not get any answers back. I've never been very good about sharing my troubles with anybody, except Tricia, and even then I'm hesitant because I don't want to bring her down.

Hunter's arrival provided a nice diversion for me at a very difficult time. I just wish I could have been in better condition to really enjoy him.

I took Hunter out in the backyard. The only way I could get him to run was to have him chase after me. So I started a light jog around the yard. It's not more than thirty or forty yards around the edge of the perimeter. I did that one time and I was pooped. So I just sat down on the ground and played with him.

It was kind of ironic. Here was this fresh, new life, so full of himself. And here I was this big guy who, less than a year earlier, was a well-conditioned athlete still clinging to the idea of getting back to the big leagues.

Now in a matter of forty-five seconds, this little puppy had worn me out. It was a nice warm day, about fifty-five degrees. A great day to be outside, but I was out of gas in no time.

By mid-January 1992, it was a struggle just to put in a half-day's work at the office. I'd go home and crawl into bed or just lay in front of the television. At that point, I knew it wasn't going to be long before I went on dialysis. Maybe then, getting all those impurities out of my blood, I'd start to feel more normal.

Then came strike three! We were visiting with Dr. Mertz in February when Tricia told him that she noticed I was sleeping erratically. I'd make these vicious snoring sounds like I was gasping for air. She told him I was thrashing around in bed a lot.

Tricia is a pretty sound sleeper, but these snoring noises I made often woke her up. It sounded to her like I wasn't breathing for periods of up to thirty seconds.

We weren't sure if this was related to the kidney problem, but we definitely thought Dr. Mertz should know about it. He referred us to a sleep disorder specialist, Dr. Ann Romaker.

She told us on our first visit (March 10, 1992) that it sounded like I had sleep apnea. I had never heard of it, but it's basically a condition when you stop breathing in your sleep and your body goes, "Hey, I need oxygen!" So it gasps for the air, which doesn't necessarily wake you up, but it keeps a person from getting to that deep, level four sleep where the body really gets its rest.

Dr. Romaker wanted to send me to a sleep lab for further tests. I just didn't know how much more of this I could take.

My body was so fatigued by then that it was a monumental chore just to get out of bed and go to the bathroom. I no longer stood to urinate. I sat. When I showered, I would sit at the bottom of the tub and wash as much of me as I could. Then I'd stand up, rinse off quickly and get to the bed to dry off. Sometimes I would just lay there to catch my breath.

It was absolutely phenomenal to simply get through a day. Doing simple things like climbing the stairs drained me. The time to go on dialysis was coming, yet I hadn't even made the decision of what type of dialysis treatment I wanted. Now I had this sleep doctor telling me to come back in for more tests.

Enough already! I just wanted to throw myself a big, ol' pity party. This was crazy. Not one, not two, but three life-threatening problems at the same time.

I remembered seeing this sign on a wall at church that said: "Do not feel totally, personally, irrevocably responsible for everything. . . .That's my job. Love, God."

OK, I thought. If this is your job, could I please get a little service around here?

In the middle of March, my condition got so bad that it was time to decide what type of dialysis treatment I wanted to receive. Hemodialysis or peritoneal dialysis? Basically, it was a matter of choosing between the lesser of two evils.

Tricia was in favor of the peritoneal method because it's something you can do at home. Since she was a nurse, she could help me and I wouldn't have to go to a clinic.

In this method, you first have to have a catheter inserted below your navel, which goes into the peritoneal lining of the stomach. You put this fluid into a tube and that helps draw out all the impurities from your blood. You empty out the bad stuff through a hose, then switch lines and fill it up with a new, fresh solution.

This process takes about forty-five minutes to an hour and must be done four times a day. The real plus with peritoneal dialysis is it's not as taxing on the body as hemodialysis, where you go to a clinic three times a week and get hooked up to a machine for four-hour treatments.

My first instinct was to try hemodialysis because I couldn't fathom the thought of having a tube hanging out of my stomach. Tricia kept telling me that nobody would see it. The tube would be covered and that it would not be uncomfortable once it was in and the incision healed.

Finally, Tricia convinced me to go with the peritoneal method. After they put the catheter in, I waited a couple of weeks for everything to heal up and I was ready to go. During the waiting period, I had to go to St. Luke's Hospital every day for training until the doctors were convinced I could properly handle doing the treatments myself.

On April 6, 1992, I began dialysis. I got my first treatment when I woke up in the morning, then repeated the process around twelve noon, again at four or five o'clock, and finally at bedtime.

Unfortunately, I ran into problems that first week. The catheter leaked, which caused non-sterile germs to get into my stomach. That lead to a common infection with this procedure called peritonitis, so I had to stop dialysis for a few days.

When I picked up again, it was time to address my sleep disorder problem. I went into the sleep lab on April 11, at which time it was discovered I was having about eight hundred apneas a night. They weren't all severe, but it was enough to keep me from getting the proper rest.

Dr. Romaker said that I was not getting the level four sleep I needed. I barely even got to level two.

To combat the problem, I was put on a C-Pap machine. That stands for Continuous Positive Airway Pressure. It provided a constant flow of continuous air while I was sleeping. It forced air into the trachea and down into the lungs to keep them open.

Now here's the tricky part: I also had to wear a mask that's connected to a hose as I'm sleeping. I could not get used to doing that. Maybe if this sleep apnea problem had popped up at a different time, like when I didn't have a million other health questions on my mind, I might have been able to deal with this funky contraption a little better.

Never mind the fact this gadget made me look like I'm going snorkeling. I wanted nothing to do with this C-Pap machine. It made it really tough to exhale. I was just learning how to do dialysis on my own without Tricia's help. I didn't want the added burden of sleeping with this stupid mask, so I just put it away.

It wasn't until after my transplant operation, when I had to go back into the sleep lab to prove that this machine didn't work for me, that I found a better alternative. They gave me a Bi-Pap machine, which is more expensive, but much easier to use because it breathes along with me.

Still, it took months for me to get remotely comfortable with the idea of wearing this equipment to bed. I looked like Jacques Cousteau preparing for an underwater exploration.

I mean, if anyone breaks into my house at night and rouses me out of bed, I won't need to reach for a gun. Just the sight of this space alien in pajamas would probably scare them into running for their life.

Around mid-April, I was told to stop driving because they were afraid I'd fall asleep at the wheel. I already had two minor accidents because I wasn't as alert as I should have been.

Fortunately, the dialysis treatments were becoming routine and I started to feel better physically. So much better that I made a trip to Denver for a New York Life meeting. I took boxes filled with these solution bags. In-between meetings, I would go up to my room for an hour and do my treatments. No problem.

I got back home Saturday night, and the next morning I attended an NFL Draft party for the Kansas City Chiefs inside their locker room. I got back home around three o'clock in the afternoon. I had just finished a dialysis procedure when the phone rang.

There was a woman on the other end. I didn't catch her name. All I heard her say was, "Would you like a kidney?" I kind of laughed for a second, figuring it was a friend pulling a joke on me. I said: "Yeah, just send it on over. Lots of pepperoni, hold the anchovies."

She then said she was serious, that she might have a kidney donor that was a match for me. I thought, "C'mon, the joke is over, who is this?" She said her name again and that she was from the Organ Procurement Agency and that they just received a kidney. There were two people on the waiting list ahead of me, but they didn't think one would be a match. The other was out of town and they'd know in the next few hours if that person could be reached.

I was told to sit by the phone and wait for a return call. Now my stomach was in knots. I just couldn't believe it. Doctors told us the average wait was twelve to eighteen months for a kidney. Some people wait years. Others never get one.

Here I had been on dialysis for only a couple of weeks and now they were telling me I might get a kidney. I phoned Tricia, who was at a friend's bridal shower, and she came home immediately.

A couple of hours later, the agency called to say they found the woman who had been out of town and she'd be tested at the hospital around nine o'clock. They felt pretty good about her being a match and they apologized for raising my hopes.

I was still pacing nervously. Tricia tried to calm me down, telling me that it was unheard of to get a kidney this quick and saying, "Let's just go to bed." We had to go to work in the morning, so I went to take a shower around 10:30 p.m.

That's when the phone rang again. Tricia answered. It was the hospital. They told Tricia to "get Ed down to the hospital right away because the kidney is his." The lady ahead of me on the waiting list wasn't a match.

You talk about an emotional roller coaster. This made the Mets' 1986 post-season look like a stroll in the park.

First you might have a kidney, then you don't, now it's yours. Wait, you still have to get tested at the hospital. Make that a definite maybe.

I got to St. Luke's about 11:30 p.m. and just shortly before one o'clock in the morning, the tests confirmed I was a match.

Now I had to catch what little sleep I could because they were going to operate first thing in the morning. Somebody came from respiratory therapy to give me a C-Pap machine. They said it was doctor's orders. I told them to take it back, that I wouldn't use the mask.

They insisted, so I told them to just leave it, but I never put the thing on. Yeah, with a kidney transplant first thing in the morning, I was going to go to bed with a mask on my face and sleep like a baby for five hours. No problem.

Are you out of your cotton-pickin' mind? Haven't you got a bedpan to change? My life was on the line the next morning and they were telling me I had to wear a mask to sleep!

Don't you love hospitals? I know, they're just doing their job.

Emotionally, this was an incredibly difficult turnaround. I should have been elated at the news of getting a donor. So many people wait years to receive a matching organ. Others die because a suitable donor is never found. The odds of getting a kidney after two weeks on dialysis were astronomical.

Still, a part of me was incredibly scared because I had mentally prepared myself to be on dialysis for quite a while. I had just gotten accustomed to doing the treatments myself. There was no time for doctors to even educate me on the transplant procedure.

Now, because of someone else's tragedy (an eighteen-year-old had been killed in a car accident) and pure luck of the draw, I'd be on the operating table in a few hours. Once a matching organ is found, it must be used as quickly as possible. The timetable varies with different organs, but it's usually within thirty or forty hours.

I can't begin to express the whirlwind of gut-wrenching emotions Tricia and I went through that night at the hospital.

Deep down, I knew that kidney represented a chance, maybe my only chance, to eventually live somewhat of a normal life. But the truth is, at that moment, I was petrified. Without Tricia, who was always so positive, I doubt that I could have prepared so quickly to make that transition from dialysis to kidney recipient.

I didn't know if I was ready for this. I guess I hadn't been on dialysis long enough to really appreciate how wonderful an opportunity I was given.

But it's too late to turn back now. You just hope and pray, mostly pray, that everything's going to be OK. All those surgeries I had before on my shoulder, and on my ears as a child, seemed like centuries ago. They seemed so easy.

This was different. We were playing for keeps now.

In times like that, you find yourself grasping for strength. Not just for words of encouragement, but anything to draw upon that will give you some kind of lift.

That's when I thought about Debbie, my younger sister, and what she went through at age fifteen. Debbie had a condition known as scoliosis, which is a curvature of the spine. She wanted to avoid surgery if at all possible, so an electronic stimulator with platinum screws was inserted into the muscles of her spine. She was only the fourth person in the world to attempt this procedure.

It's similar to a heart pacemaker. It's connected to a radio apparatus that was kept by her bed. When she slept, it gave her a mild shock about every ten seconds. You could actually see her twitch in her sleep.

For a while, this procedure seemed to work, but one of those screws came loose and doctors gave her the option of another implant or surgery. She chose the implant, but it failed, so they had to operate.

This was an excruciating time for our family. It was right after my rookie league season with the Phillies and I was rehabilitating my shoulder at spring training in Clearwater. It killed me not to be with them.

The operation was done at Jackson Memorial Hospital in Miami. It involved shaving all the bumps of the bone off Debbie's back, plus taking bone from her hip and making these match-stick-sized pieces out of it to lay on top of the sawed-off bone. Doctors also inserted a Harrington rod, about the size of your pinkie finger, along the spine to make sure the back remained per-fectly still.

Debbie went through unbelievable pain. Not only that, she had to wear a body cast from her neck to the bottom of her spine for six months, which meant she couldn't even shower that whole time.

The timing for Debbie was awful. She was a sophomore at Fort Pierce Westwood High School, which had just opened that year, and already had her sights set on being class valedictorian. She was also a cheerleader and her boyfriend at the time had already asked her to the prom, which was two months after the surgery.

Suddenly, Debbie was confronted with the real possibility of losing out on the goals and activities that she cherished the most. It was frightening enough for me to think about at age thirty-one. Imagine what it must have felt like at fifteen.

But Debbie's ambition, determination and family support got her through that ordeal. She went to that prom in a special dress that Mom made for her so the body cast wouldn't show. It was a peach-colored skirt with four tiers that hid the parts where Debbie's cast protruded out.

When football season came around, the doctors told Debbie she could only attempt what she felt she was physically capable of doing. Well, she cheered in another special outfit that covered up the body cast until it was removed midway through the season.

Academically, Debbie fell behind, but she eventually caught up after getting home-bound instruction for four months. She graduated as the class valedictorian. Not once, but twice. The first time with Westwood in 1981 and again at Indian River Community College two years later.

Debbie, who lives in Orlando with her husband, Tim Shannon, and 16-month-old son, Jack (named after our grandfather), went on to a successful sales career with IBM. She now works in an exciting position with the new sports development division of Walt Disney World.

I regret not being able to be with Debbie when she went through major surgery, but she was definitely with me in spirit when I went through mine.

Just knowing she made it back, and was a stronger person for it, was an inspiration at a time when I felt rather desperate.

On April 27, 1992, my life forever changed. I received a healthy kidney. They call it a transplant, but there's no trade involved. Yes, you get an organ from another body, but they don't remove your non-functioning kidneys. They simply put a new one inside you.

So I have three kidneys. It's just that only one of them works.

The operation took about four hours and things appeared to go well, but there was no way of knowing for sure how well the kidney was going to do. I would have to give it some time.

They kept me in the recovery room for over twenty-four hours. I just couldn't move because of this sharp pain in my stomach. It's been four years and I've still got a fourteen-inch inch scar that runs from a few inches below my navel to one-third of the way up my torso.

I was a little puzzled when I first woke up from surgery because Tricia wasn't there as she promised. I didn't know that they would not let her in the room.

When Tricia finally saw me, she said she could understand why they didn't let her in. Apparently, I looked so bad that she thought I was dead. I was yellow and real waxy-looking.

The pain was intense those first few days, but I had my morphine button to push whenever I wanted it. Still, that button couldn't deaden the pain going through my mind.

About the third night there, I was lying awake and thinking about all that's happened in the last few months. I started having one of those pity parties, as I like to call them.

Just thinking about it being April and how former teammates were back on the field making big money, doing what I used to do. I was thinking about how life threw me this wicked, nasty curve ball that I didn't deserve.

I was scared. I didn't know what I was going to be able to do in the future. What kind of life was I going to be able to lead? How could I make a living to provide for my wife? Would we ever be able to have kids?

Being in the hospital does that. You've got all this time and if you're not seeing visitors, the only thing a bed-ridden patient can do is eat, watch television or think.

Well, that night I was thinking about what a crummy hand I had been dealt. As I was doing this, a nurse walked in from the midnight shift.

She saw that I was awake, so she asked me how come I wasn't asleep. I was in no mood to play twenty questions, so I smugly replied: "What's it to ya?"

Then she asked me if I was feeling sorry for myself. Again, I said: "What's it to ya?"

I can barely remember what this nurse looked like. I never got her name, but I'll never forget what she did next. She proceeded to tell me a story about the man who felt bad about the shoes he wore until he met another man who had no feet.

Whenever I speak today, I challenge people with that story because it's so true. That nurse made me realize there were a lot of people out there worse off than I was.

I was very lucky to have a wife that cared for me. Lucky to be able to afford the kind of quality doctors that treated me. Lucky to have played baseball as long as I did and been part of a World Series championship team. Most of all, I was lucky I wasn't dying.

Sometimes when you least expect it, and when you're in the greatest need, God sends a messenger to hit you right between the eyes.

For the rest of my hospital stay, my spirits picked up a bit. I was determined to get better.

Instead of just lying in bed, I made a more conscious effort to get up and walk. The first time is very painful, but I slowly felt my strength coming back. Pretty soon, I was walking twenty yards down the hall, then all the way around the corner.

Before I left, I was playing putt-putt in the halls and visiting other patients, including someone else who had a transplant.

I heard about a kid in the pediatric ward who had been in a car accident, so I made it a point to go see him. I had to wear this mask so I wouldn't pick up infections because of my weak immune system. I signed an autograph for him and just tried to encourage him, let him know he was not alone. I don't know if I helped him, but it sure helped me. My attitude was a lot better after that visit.

My blood work was improving every day, too. Glenn Ezell, the Kansas City Royals' bullpen coach, came up to visit on behalf of the team. The cards, plants and flowers I received from friends and family were overwhelming. I could feel myself bouncing back, eager to join the real world again.

Tricia brought Hunter to the hospital and I was allowed to take him outside on the hospital grounds. She would bring a picnic lunch. Tricia, Hunter and I would sit around and chow down.

Things were finally looking up. After seven days in the hospital (most kidney transplant recipients stay ten to fourteen days), they sent me home.

I was on the road to recovery. Or so it seemed.

The Inside Pitch

The Gift of Life

*"Don't take your organs to heaven; heaven knows
we need them here."*

I shudder to think about the number of times each day that Americans, in the process of getting or renewing their driver's license, fail to take a moment to consider signing the back of it and commit to being an organ donor. If only they realized how valuable this gesture could be.

As the years pass and medical technology continues to develop, the success rates of transplant surgery have improved remarkably. Transplantation is one of the most remarkable success stories in the history of medicine. In most cases, it's the only hope for thousands of people suffering from organ failure, or in desperate need of corneas, skin, bone or other tissue.

Yet, there remains a major challenge. A growing shortage exists in the supply of organs and tissue available for transplantation. Many Americans who need transplants cannot get them because of these shortages. The result is that many of these people die while waiting for that "Gift of Life."

Each year, several national organizations develop special public education programs aimed at increasing public awareness of the need for organ and tissue donation. One such group is the National Kidney Foundation. Besides the usual work of spreading the word by way of public forums and literature, the NKF coordinates a wonderful event called the United States Transplant Games.

Held every other year, these games bring together a wide variety of transplant recipients. These twelve hundred recipient/athletes range from those who were transplanted as long as twenty years ago to those who will have received a transplant just months before the event.

By competing in such events as track and field, bicycling, tennis and swimming, these transplant athletes demonstrate to the world that those who are given a "second chance at life" can and do return to full, productive lives. One such athlete is Greg Wright from Kansas City. Within a short couple of years after a liver transplant, he began competing in marathons and mini-triathlons. Recently he ran the New York City Marathon, just missing the qualifying time for the Boston Marathon by a few minutes!

The Transplant Games are also an opportunity to recognize and pay tribute to the more than four thousand American families who donate the organs and tissue of their family members every year. While doing this, the games also help increase awareness and support for organ donation.

Educating the public about organ and tissue donation helps everyone make an informed decision about this very important issue. Obviously, this subject lies very close to my heart and therefore I'd like to share with you some brief facts that might encourage you to consider one day giving this wonderful gift:

* Every twenty minutes, another name is added to the transplant waiting list.
* Eight people die every day without ever receiving the life-saving transplant they need.
* Almost anyone can be an organ, tissue or eye donor.
* One donor can save and enhance the lives of over seventy-five people.

Baseball great Mickey Mantle, who last year was a liver recipient, made national headlines across the country as he led a courageous drive to increase organ donor awareness. Sadly, he passed away, succumbing finally to cancer two months after he had received his gift of life. But the impact he has had on organ donor awareness was incredible.

He was a man who was a hero to many young boys during the 1950s. More importantly, he could be an unsung hero to many others in the future as a result of his efforts in encouraging others to sign their donor cards.

Another unsung hero, Robert Noel Test, has really touched my heart with the following composition:

TO REMEMBER ME

At a certain moment a doctor will determine that my brain has ceased to function and that, for all intents and purposes, my life has stopped.

When that happens, do not attempt to instill artificial life into my body by the use of a machine. And don't call this my "deathbed." Call it my "bed of life" and let my body be taken from it to help others lead fuller lives.

Give my sight to a man who has never seen a sunrise, a baby's face or the love in the eyes of a woman.

Give my heart to a person whose own heart has caused nothing but endless days of pain.

Give my blood to the teenager who has been pulled from the wreckage of his car, so that he might live to see his grandchildren play.

Give my kidneys to one who depends on a machine to exist from week to week.

Take my bones, every muscle, every fiber and nerve in my body and find a way to make a crippled child walk.

Explore every corner of my brain. Take my cells, if necessary, and let them grow so that someday a speechless boy will shout at the crack of a bat and a deaf girl will hear the sound of rain against her window.

Burn what is left of me and scatter the ashes to the winds to help the flowers grow.

If you must bury something, let it be my faults, my weaknesses and all my prejudice against my fellow man.

Give my soul to God.

If by chance you wish to remember me, do it with a kind deed or word to someone who needs you.

And if you do all I have asked, I will live forever.

Isn't that awesome? Now here's my challenge to you. Right

now, turn to the back of this book where you will find an organ donor card. Stop and think for a moment about the possibility of some day giving many others like me a second chance at life.

If you feel moved to accept this wonderful opportunity, fill out the card and sign your name. Then, most importantly, share your decision with other members of your family. This will assure that if the occasion should ever arise where you are in a position to be considered a candidate for organ donation, your family can share your wishes and desires with the medical staff.

My friend, if you have accepted this challenge, all the time and effort I have put into the writing of this book will have been well worth the trouble. I thank you from the bottom of my heart.

14

3-D World:
Darkness, Despair, Doubt

*C*oming home after my kidney transplant, especially those first couple of weeks, I was as excited as I had been in a long time. The challenges ahead were a bit frightening, but the anticipation of feeling better in time uplifted me.

Physically, I had a long way to go, but my mental frame of mind was positive. There was definitely a carry-over effect from my last few days in the hospital. It didn't matter so much what condition my shoes were in. I just wanted to run the race and feel alive again.

Just let me be an everyday nine-to-five working stiff. Let me laugh. Let me wince at a missed putt. Let me hunt. Let me cry. Let me go through one day without wondering if this medical merry-go-round will ever end.

But I guess some things, for whatever reason, just aren't meant to be that simple. The hurdles just kept on coming.

Four weeks after the transplant, I was back in St. Luke's Hospital for a biopsy, which determined that my body was starting to reject the new kidney. Transplant recipients are given what they call immunosuppressive drugs to help the body adjust to the additional organ, but they don't always work. No matter how well a donor kidney matches up in preliminary tests, there is no guarantee of smooth sailing after the new organ is put in.

I was given a new drug called OKT3, which was the last major piece of ammunition to prevent my body from rejecting the kidney. About a half-hour after that IV, I was sitting in my hospital bed watching television and started to feel a chill. So I reached down to pull the sheets over me.

All of a sudden, I got these violent shivers. It was extremely intense. Then I experienced shortness of breath and my chest started hurting. The cardiac unit was alerted and came into my room as a precautionary measure.

What happened was I had a bad reaction to the OKT3 medication. For the next forty-eight hours, I ran a high fever. It got so bad that they put me on a cooling mattress, which ran cold water through it to help get my body temperature down.

I finally went home after a week in the hospital, but that episode proved to be the first in a long series of post-transplant setbacks that almost did me in permanently.

For the rest of that summer, I felt like a vegetable. Just totally lethargic. No energy. No get-up-and-go. No ambition to do much beyond sleeping and lying in front of the television.

Not that I expected to be working regular hours by then, but I wasn't seeing the kind of physical progress that I had hoped for and it started to affect my mental outlook as well.

One thing I remember vividly in June 1992, was getting permission from the doctor to hit some golf balls at a local driving range. Nothing strenuous. It wasn't like I pulled out a Big Bertha driver and started whaling away. This was just some light hitting with wedges and some short irons.

To my amazement, I could barely make any connection with the ball. It was like I never played golf before. This really floored me. I carried about a five handicap when I played on a regular basis. I knew I was worn down, but I looked worse than a beginner on that range and thought to myself: "God, I'll never be right again."

About the same time I had trouble hitting a golf ball, I did get hit by cytomegalovirus, CMV for short, which is an ailment not uncommon to transplant recipients. I was on all kinds of medication and my immune system was being suppressed so it wouldn't attack and reject my new kidney. This left me susceptible to all kinds of viruses.

Well, this CMV knocked me for a loop. Every day for two months, I had diarrhea and a low-grade fever. Every day! No matter what I drank, ate or how much I rested, the condition would not go away. I felt as weak as I did in the weeks leading up to dialysis.

I finally had to go back into the hospital for dehydration. Since it was mostly IV treatments, they let me go after three days because Tricia could administer them to me at home.

But the sobering truth about my condition, physically and mentally, was I was in a downward spiral. I didn't feel like doing anything. I rarely attempted to make calls to drum up business for New York Life. Nothing moved me.

Actually, I shouldn't say nothing moved me because duck-hunting was my one refuge in the fall of '92. I was too weak to walk the fields for quail and pheasant. Forget climbing a tree to get into a deer stand. But I could sit in a duck blind. The few times I did go were like finding an oasis in the middle of a desert.

Once hunting season stopped, I felt I had nothing to really keep me going. That CMV virus really zapped me. Between that, combined with the uncertainty of getting better and the side effects of all the medication I was on, I found myself gradually slipping into a depressive state. This is not uncommon. Often times, the immunosuppressive medications can cause a chemical imbalance in the brain which can lead to depression.

It was like my world turned shades of black and white. The color was gone. I used to be a pretty emotional guy. I wasn't one of those guys that thought crying was for sissies. Before the transplant, I could cry tears of joy, happiness, sadness. I don't know why, but I noticed after the operation that I could not cry anymore, even though there were times I really needed to.

Life had lost its meaning. I could function, but I had no drive to be productive.

I started putting on a lot of weight because of my inactivity and the Prednisone, which was a steroid I took as part of my medical treatment. Some people put on eighty to one hundred pounds after a transplant and I was getting up in that ball park (I'm about eighty pounds above my baseball-playing weight today).

Over the Christmas holidays, Tricia and I had gone back to New York to visit her family. She grew up on Long Island with her German-born parents, Heinz and Ursula, and her younger brother, Thomas. I usually call them Mutti and Vati, which is German for Mom and Dad. They had prepared a true family Christmas, complete with a beautiful nativity scene, festive decorations and a delicious feast of goodies. Yet, my mood was anything but upbeat.

Thomas, a civil engineer for the New York State Department of Transportation, tried to amuse me with all kinds of explanations for the massive amounts of road construction, detours and potholes. I laughed on the outside, but that didn't change the way I felt on the inside.

We all went out on Christmas Eve to look at light displays. When we got back, my parents were waiting in a rental car.

Mom and Dad often surprised me in the minor leagues by showing up sooner than they said they were coming, but this visit was totally unexpected. I was really glad to see them. It really lifted my spirits, at least temporarily, but inside I continued struggling with depression.

I put on a good front for everyone while we were together. It was Christmas and regardless of how I felt, I did not want to ruin the holidays for everyone by dumping all my problems on them. They probably knew I wasn't feeling great, but I don't think they realized how low my morale had sunk.

It was hard to be around people and put on that facade, acting as if everything was fine when I really felt like crap. Of course, the one person I never did this with was Tricia.

But, during my depressed state, I did one of the worst things a person could ever do to someone who loves them. I would constantly put myself down in front of her, often saying things like: "Just take me out behind the barn and shoot me."

She would tell me to stop feeling sorry for myself, which is exactly what I was doing, but I never really stopped to consider the impact of those statements.

It did not dawn on me when I said that I wasn't worth caring for anymore how much I was really hurting my partner. Tricia told me: "Gosh, do you think my love for you is so shallow that I shouldn't care for you when you're sick? That's when true love is at its peak."

Tricia had to lower the boom on me a few times about that. She sympathized with my physical and emotional struggles, but she did not appreciate me wallowing in self-pity.

I'm just glad I pulled myself together before I let this depression thing get too deep. Believe me, I pushed it about as far as I could go without paying the ultimate price.

Around early March 1993, I had hit rock bottom. My physical condition was a little better, but I couldn't shake the constant state of despair in my mind.

This wasn't the best time of year for me to be feeling down and out. Hunting season was over and baseball season was about to crank up. It just put more negative thoughts in my head.

When I was in that negative mode, I never saw the glass as half-full. It was always half-empty.

I started thinking about many of my former teammates and instead of being happy that they were still playing, I found myself resenting their good fortune. It was particularly hard to listen to guys talk about how tough it was with all the economic changes that were taking place in baseball. "Golly, I'm only going to make $1.5 million next year instead of the $2 million I should be getting."

Listen buddy. You'd better find somebody else's shoulder to cry on.

Sometimes I'd say to myself: "It's not right. What have I done to deserve this? Guys I know are still making millions of dollars playing a kids' game, some of them party animals and cheating on their wives. Here I am, one of the good guys, and I'm getting raked over the coals. Why?"

This is a terrible thing to have to admit, but that's the kind of stuff that went through my mind at those low moments.

One day, while Tricia was at work, I went down to our basement and picked up a .357 Magnum. I started contemplating a pretty horrifying act. I put a bullet in one of the chambers. I never pointed it at myself or did the Russian roulette thing, but I was definitely having suicidal thoughts.

I could understand how Donnie Moore, the late California Angels pitcher, could get to the point where he felt life was no longer worth living. In fact, research done at the University of Southern Maine in the late 1980s discovered that seventy-seven big leaguers had taken their lives, most of them after leaving the game.

I don't know if it was a reflex, a wake-up call or what, but I finally realized what I was considering here. It scared the heck out of me.

Deep down, I was not a quitter. That was not in my makeup. I spent my entire pro baseball career sticking it out in the worst times.

I've got a loving wife and family that cares for me deeply. What in the world was I thinking in that basement? Whatever it was, I had to snap out of it fast.

One of the first things I did after that gun incident was take all my hunting firearms out of that basement. I had a key to a neighbor's house and his basement was such a mess, I knew I could hide the guns down there and nobody would ever notice them.

If I ever had thoughts like that again, I just wanted to eliminate the temptation of the guns being so easily accessible. I left them there for about four or five months. My neighbor still doesn't know I hid them there.

I told Tricia about what I did with the guns and she took it rather well. Not that it wasn't uncomfortable to hear, but she understood more than anybody the pain I was going through. I think she was just glad I confronted the situation and attempted to do something to change it. That is, if you call moving guns from one basement to another down the street a change.

Maybe it wasn't a real change, but at least it wasn't the end.

When I look back on it now, I don't think I really wanted to end my life. More than anything, I just wanted people to understand how bad I was feeling.

During that time, I was putting on this facade of strength for people. I tried to be strong for everybody else outside of Tricia, but

I was torn apart inside.

My thoughts that day were more like wishing I could somehow splatter myself all over the walls, step back behind the corner and observe people saying: "Gosh, I didn't know he was hurting this badly." Then, I'd come back into the scene, show people I was really alive and they could help me.

From that day on, I made a conscious effort to try to do what I could to snap out of this funk. Things like this are never as easy as flipping on a light switch, but I had to take some action.

Three things helped me get back on track. First, I got some psychiatric counseling. Dr. Mertz, the nephrologist who oversaw my kidney transplant, put me in touch with Dr. Scott Jones, who specialized in dealing with depression and had worked at the prestigious Menninger Clinic.

I started seeing Dr. Jones three times a week in June 1993, and kept having sessions with him periodically through November 1994. He really helped me in different ways, but most importantly, it gave me someone else to dump my problems on. You can't be dumping on your spouse all the time.

Second, I took a cue from my early training at New York Life and started listening to audio cassette tapes with positive messages. When you go through insurance training programs, they encourage you to listen to motivational tapes of top sales people and I just felt that if I forced myself to start doing this, it might take hold.

Many a night, I would fall asleep listening to motivational speakers like Zig Ziglar, Earl Nightingale and Dr. Norman Vincent Peale. I became a cassette-tape junkie. That helped because it got positive energy flowing into my mind instead of cluttering it with all that negative baggage I had been carrying around.

Lastly, and most important of all, I had to draw on the one thing that I could never lose: my faith. No matter what, even at the worst possible moments, I believed God would never totally abandon me.

I may have misplaced Him at times, forgotten about Him at times, but I always believed He was there for me. All I had to do was reach out to Him.

God had given me so many wonderful things in my life. A devoted wife, loving parents, a supportive family, the rewards of hard work, the courage to endure my trials.

Now it was up to me to ask for more strength to deal with the difficult road ahead. It's right there in Philippians 4:13, one of the most widely quoted Scripture passages of all time. It's so true: "I can do all things through Christ who strengthens me."

That is one of the most powerful comforts for anyone facing difficult challenges. If nothing else, that verse right there told me that I had the power to snap out of this depression. All I had to do was hang on to my faith. It's like that final knot on the end of a rope, which is always the strongest.

In the spring of '93, I had no idea what I would do with the rest of my life. I just knew somehow I had to keep plugging away and give God a chance to make me whole again.

There's an excerpt from the fictional novel *The Screwtape Letters,* by C.S. Lewis, that really describes my state of mind at the time. Uncle Screwtape, the devil's under-secretary, is giving advice to his nephew, Wormwood, a tempter assigned the task of bringing the devil more clients.

He writes to Wormwood: "Do not be deceived. Our cause is never more endangered than when a human, no longer desiring or intending to do our enemy's (God's) will, looks around upon the universe and every trace of Him seems to have vanished and he asks why he has been forsaken. And then still obeys."

That is just about where Ed Hearn was at. I was weak. I was human. But I hung on to that last knot on the rope.

Except for a little more positive attitude, nothing much changed through the summer of '93. I continued seeing Dr. Jones for my depression and my physical condition stabilized a little bit.

I wasn't ready to play eighteen holes of golf, but I had some days where my energy level showed signs of getting better. At least I felt the urge again to go out and do some things.

In September, I got a call from Dave Lindstrom, a former Kansas City Chiefs player who owns a couple of Burger Kings in the area. He was a member of the Overland Park Rotary Club and wanted to know if I'd be a guest speaker.

It was the usual deal. You eat lunch, watch the club do their business and then talk for about twenty minutes. I spoke about my roller coaster baseball career and the turbulent times I faced after it was over.

This talk wasn't much different from others I'd given in my baseball days to youth groups, Fellowship of Christian Athletes or anyone else. It had been a while since I did one, but the people there that day seemed to enjoy it. I got many compliments.

The president of the club that year was Brad Plumb, who sat at the head table and nonchalantly handed me his business card. He said I had a great story and, for a jock, I told it well. Plumb also happens to run the North American Speakers Bureau.

He told me when we got together for lunch at a later date that I had a compelling message and that corporate America would pay me to share that with their people. That was flattering, but inside I was still battling the depression and I thought: "How can I empower others when I can barely empower myself?"

Still, I remember going home that day and feeling pretty upbeat. Not that I had any intentions of jumping into a speaking career, but it was nice to hear all that positive feedback.

Brad advised me that if I had any interest in speaking, he would help me organize some material and put a package together. I kept it in mind, but just went about my business. I got busy with New York Life stuff, kept trying to climb out of the depression and, basically, just getting my life together again.

When the holidays arrived, I was in much better spirits. I was still overweight, still prone to days of minimal energy, but I definitely felt like a different person from the man who walked around in a fog for most of the year.

That Christmas, Tricia and I would have even more reason to celebrate.

We went down to Florida to visit my parents, then made the fifty-mile drive on Christmas day to this beach house in Melbourne. That night, Tricia and I went for a walk along the beach. It was just after sunset, a beautiful night.

As we got to a point where we started turning back, we stopped for a quick hug. Nothing real mushy, but a nice romantic moment.

Then Tricia said: "What would you think if I told you that we were gonna have a baby?" Pause. A few seconds of silence. I asked if she was serious and Tricia said: "I think I might be."

Tricia's suspicions were raised the day before, so she went to the drug store that afternoon and got a home pregnancy test. It came up positive, but she wanted to wait until we were alone to tell me. There was never a good time with my family around.

Another concern Tricia had was how I might react to the news. We had been married six years and though I always wanted kids, part of me was a bit skeptical at the time. I was still struggling a little bit and trying to get on my feet.

But if you always wait for the perfect moment, you might end up not having any kids at all. I was genuinely excited about the idea of becoming a father. It was scary, but scary in a good way.

If I needed any further incentive to keep battling back, this was certainly the kind of kick to get me going.

The Inside Pitch

Faith

"Peace is seeing a sunrise or sunset and knowing Who to thank."

Have you ever sat on a beach and watched the early morning sunrise? Have you ever climbed to the top of a mountain and enjoyed the last rays of sunshine as the day comes to an end? Fortunately, being an outdoorsman, I've had many opportunities to enjoy these beautiful times. I also am very fortunate to know whom to thank for these and every other moment of my life—Our Heavenly Father.

As a young boy I was raised in a family atmosphere that nurtured the development of a faith in our Creator. Every night before we went to bed, my Mom would read us stories from a children's Bible or a testimony from one of the many Fellowship of Christian Athlete books she often brought home.

This laid the foundation for me to learn about and begin to develop my own faith. I was particularly receptive to the professional athletes who openly shared their faith.

One such player was Norm Evans, a former All-Pro offensive tackle with the Miami Dolphins. One day when I was ten-years-old, my parents took me down to the Dolphins training camp in south Florida. I stood anxiously waiting for the players to leave the practice field in hopes that I could get a few autographs.

Finally, they started to head right past me going to the locker room. That's when this huge man stopped and reached for my pen and paper. I wasn't even sure who he was, but I was certainly excited that he stopped.

When I got home, I was admiring the signatures that I had collected. As I looked at the Norm Evans autograph, I noticed it had a word and some numbers below his name. I had to ask my parents what it meant. Dad told me it was a Bible verse—Romans 1:16: "For I am not ashamed of the gospel of Christ. For it is the powerful method of bringing salvation to all who believe it. . . ."

Wow, was I ever impressed! Here was a bigger-than-life pro football player who took the extra time to instill in me the same values that my parents stressed.

Ironically, some seventeen years later, I met Norm for a second time during the Royals' spring training. This time, I was the professional athlete and I had the opportunity to touch his life. I shared with him the story about him signing that autograph for me and how I had never forgotten it. I even quoted it to him right there on the spot.

He was very moved by my story and then told me about the ministry he was heading up for professional athletes. The following off-season, I, former Royals' third baseman Kevin Seitzer, and our wives all attended a conference that was held in Orlando, Florida, by Norm's ministry called Pro Athletes Outreach. As it turned out, that conference was a big stepping stone in the development of my Christian faith.

It was this faith that, over the past eight years of challenging times, has been like a light at the end of a very long and dark tunnel. But, I have to be honest here. There were some instances when I was ready to throw in the towel. Why me, Lord?

Much like the writers of the book of Psalms, I let my feelings of despair be known to God on more than one occasion. There were times when I wanted to get down on my knees, pick up the red phone, dial the 1-800 direct line to God and tell Him: "Hey, listen, Big Guy. You promised you'd never send us more than we can handle, right? Well, in case you haven't noticed, I've had just about all I can take. Can we please stop dumping on Ed now?

Oh yes, and then there is that part in Scripture (Romans 8:28) where He promises us "that all things work together for the good of those who love Him..." I can just hear myself back then responding back to God with words similar to those made famous by a recent popular television advertisement: "I LOVE YOU, MAN!"

Yes, I certainly loved God, but I was sure wondering what good could ever come out of these horrifying circumstances. But there was this faith in God I had developed over the years which stayed with me through it all, even though at times it seemed to hide way down deep inside. So deep, that at times I questioned whether it really existed.

Yet, when my life hit its deepest valley that afternoon in my basement with the .357 Magnum in my hand, it was this faith that was the "knot at the end of the rope" to which I clung. For when everything else around me was crumbling, I sensed the Hand of God reaching out to comfort me.

How shallow our human faith can get sometimes. But just when we think we're down to our last ounce, I have found that God steps in and begins to show us the light.

It took me quite a while to realize what God had planned for me. But finally, one night in the fall of 1994 while I was sitting with a small group of friends from church, I began to get the feeling He was starting to reveal to me what the game plan was for me. It all began to happen as I read a verse of scripture from II Corinthians where the Apostle Paul was talking about a tremendous revelation that he had been shown by God that could have tempted him to become boastful and full of pride:

"I will say this: because these experiences were so tremendous, God was afraid I might be puffed up about them; so I was given a thorn in the flesh to prick my pride...Three times I begged God to make me well again. Each time He said, 'No, but I am with you; that is all you need. My strength shows up best in weak people.' No I am glad to boast about how weak I am. I am glad to be a living demonstration of Christ's power, instead of showing off my own abilities. For when I am weak, then I am strong — the less I have the more I depend on Him."

From that night on, I slowly began to see what God had in mind for Ed Hearn. Today, through a series of events, I have finally realized what God had in mind for me through all those challenges.

Do you remember the gentleman named Brad Plumb who had heard me speak at the local Rotary Club? Do you recall that he said I had a great story and that I could have a very positive impact on so many peoples' lives as a professional speaker? Well, it was finally beginning to make sense to me.

Today, because of "the thorn in my flesh," I have the opportunity to go around the country sharing with thousands of people, my story and the lessons of life He has taught me. During the first two years of professional speaking, I have had the chance to touch more lives than I could have if I had played 20 years in the big leagues!

I believe He has greatness planned for all of us. But His plan may not be exactly what we have in mind for our own lives. It sure wasn't for mine! But, I speak from experience, if you let Him, He will work wonders with your life!

Yes, He did work wonders in my life as a member of that 1986 World Championship team, the New York Mets, and I have the honor to proudly wear a World Series Championship ring as a symbol of what I once thought was the greatest thrill a man could have. But believe me friends, the World Series and my days as major-league player are nothing compared to the thrill of having a personal relationship with God through Jesus Christ.

I wasn't ever going to play baseball again. Yet little did I know how much I would enjoy traveling around the country, being paid to inspire and encourage other people. Never could I have imagined this to be so personally rewarding. So rewarding, in fact, that I would come to the realization that I actually looked forward to speaking more than I used to look forward to playing in a major league game.

We of so little faith! But I have found, in time, God will reveal the greatness He has in store for all those who believe and hold firm to their faith.

In the words of this beautiful prayer: "Lord, I ain't what I ought to be. I ain't what I want to be. I ain't what I'm gonna be. But thank God, I ain't what I used to be."

15

Comeback Player
of the Year

*T*ricia's pregnancy was like a slap in the face. It told me: "Hey, you'd better shake yourself and get it together. Things are happening here. No time to feel sorry for yourself now."

Knowing I was going to become a father was one of the things that really helped me climb out of the depression. I had no choice. I had to be productive, especially with an extended family to support.

Physically, I was doing what I had to do to stay alive, but all the medication still wasn't enough to keep the disease that attacked my old kidneys from attacking my new one.

As my creatinine began to rise again early in 1994, the doctors asked me to come in for another kidney biopsy. This revealed that the disease which had damaged my own kidneys was now recurring in my new one.

So on January 27, 1994, I went back into the hospital for one last shot at trying to prevent my good kidney from degenerating. I was given a treatment called plasmapheresis, which was a fairly new technique. Dr. Mertz told me that transplant patients at the University of Kansas Medical Center had tried it and some were showing improvement.

It's almost like a dialysis treatment. But, instead of removing the impurities from your blood, this process involves taking out your blood and separating the plasma from the red blood cells. The plasma is discarded and replaced with a protein called albumin, in hopes that the antibodies causing the disease will be removed.

But after three months of these treatments, test results showed little change in my functioning kidney. What this means is that in another five or six years, I'll likely have to go back on dialysis and wait for another kidney donor. It's hard to pinpoint for sure how long my transplanted kidney will last, but doctors estimate mine is probably good for about 10 years from the time it was put in.

Despite the bad news, the impact of knowing I'll someday have to go through this all over again, I handled it better this time. I didn't let it get me down or defeat all the progress I had made in the previous months.

Tricia and I were going to have our first child. I couldn't let the challenges of my physical condition negatively impact Tricia during pregnancy, which should be a time of joy and anticipation.

Maybe it was the urgency created by the baby, maybe it was just being in a better frame of mind, maybe both, but I started pushing myself more. No matter what it took, I was determined to make a life for my family.

I remembered what Brad Plumb told me several months earlier about public speaking. If I was interested, I should put some brochures together. It was going to cost $550 to get about five hundred of them for distribution. That was a fair amount of money to us at that time. I wasn't sure if we'd make enough to break even by year's end, but Tricia gave me her blessing.

So we got the brochures to Brad at North American Speakers Bureau and to Nancy Lauterbach at Five Star Speakers Bureau in Kansas City. At that point, I envisioned doing a few speaking engagements here and there just to supplement our income. Nothing major.

Word got out that I wanted to be a speaker and my first paid engagement was on March 15, 1994, at Shawnee Heights High School in Topeka, Kansas. Shortly before then, a woman named Karen Woods, who was the sister-in-law of former major league pitcher Mike Boddicker, gave me my first booking with MCI in Sergeant Bluff, Iowa. Karen also got me another MCI engagement that spring in Iowa City.

The talk in Iowa City on May 26th was my first speech before a major company. There were a couple hundred people there and my presentation lasted about forty-five minutes.

At that time, I was very rough around the edges as a speaker. I'm sure people weren't dazzled by my skills. But in talking to them afterwards, that didn't seem to matter as much as knowing that I spoke from the heart and shared a message they could all relate to.

By the end of that summer, after I had done about fifteen engagements, I became more intrigued about pursuing this as a second career. It wasn't just the money. Being paid to speak was nice, especially since this came along at a time in our lives when the extra income really helped.

What I discovered more than anything else was how speaking had become a real rehabilitation for me. It gave me a feeling that I was doing something worthwhile and people appreciated it.

Being a former athlete, I also enjoyed being in the spotlight again. It's gratifying to be looked up to as somebody special.

Any professional athlete who says they don't miss that when they leave the game is lying. That's one of the toughest adjustments for a lot of players. How many jobs are there in the real world where people applaud as you're working? That's a high almost impossible to recapture.

As a speaker, I've had the opportunity to do that. More importantly, it makes you accountable in your own life.

If you don't live your words, then your message has no credibility. Speaking forced me whenever I'd get a little down to say: "Hey, you can't just talk the talk. You've got to walk the walk."

It was like a push to stay on track. We all need that push once in a while.

One of the greatest moments of my life was going back to the hospital on August 29, 1994. Only this time, Tricia was the patient and I was the delivery coach.

Tricia started having labor pains after midnight and she finally woke me up around three o'clock. She wanted to wait until the last possible minute before going to the hospital. We ended up getting to St. Joseph Health Center in Kansas City a couple of hours later.

Only a little while longer and the secret I had kept from Tricia for almost three months would be out.

From the very beginning, Tricia didn't want to know whether it was a boy or girl. She forbid me to try to find out because she was afraid I couldn't keep a secret. Well, that right there was an open challenge to do just the opposite.

One day, we went in to have a sonogram done and Tricia had to go to the rest room, leaving me alone in another room with a technician. Tricia left strict instructions with everyone not to say anything about the sex of the child.

During the sonogram, I started making remarks about the baby's groin area, though I actually had no idea what I was looking at. I'd say stuff like: "Oh, look at that! There it is. Look at that stem!"

I was trying to get a reaction from the technician that would give it away, but she was very careful not to slip up. But when Tricia went to the rest room, I said to the technician, "OK, what is it?" Finally, she said: "You really want to know?"

Suddenly, I could feel a tail growing out from my behind and little horns popping up on my head. I said: "Yeah, tell me." She told me it was a boy and I was just blown away. All of Tricia's friends insisted she was carrying a girl.

Right up until the time he was born, Tricia didn't think I knew. Still, I wanted to prove to her I did because she never believed I could keep a secret that long.

So I made up a sign that said "It's a boy" and gave it to a neighbor a couple of days beforehand. I also took a baby-sized New York Mets uniform and had our last name stitched on the back and snuck it into Tricia's closet at the hospital.

Shortly before noon, Tricia started pushing and almost immediately, you could see the crown of the baby's head. There was just one problem. The doctor hadn't arrived yet, so Tricia had to stop pushing for about fifteen minutes until he got there.

When Tricia started pushing again, I thought I'd bring a little levity to the occasion, so I took out my mitt and crouched into a catcher's stance in-between contractions. I placed the mitt right where the baby would come out. The hospital employees all had a good laugh. Dr. Paul Riekhof, Tricia's obstetrician, played the role of umpire behind me. He has a blown-up picture of that in his office. I signed it: "Safe at home. Good call, Doc."

Finally, at 12:19 p.m., we had a healthy boy. He weighed in at eight pounds, two ounces and measured twenty-one inches long. Now we had to decide what to name him.

Almost all the names Tricia picked out were for girls. We had already settled on Carter, after Gary Carter, as the middle name. I wanted my son to carry the name of my former teammate who I greatly admire as a person, family man and friend.

I liked Dusty for a first name because I thought it was a ballplayer's name, but after seeing the baby, he just looked like a Cody. Everyone seemed to like Cody better than Dusty, so it was settled. Cody Carter Hearn. If I say so myself, he looked pretty sharp in that Mets uniform.

Holding my son in my arms for the first time, I was finally able to do something I hadn't done in almost three years. I cried.

It's almost as if two new lives came into the world that day—Cody's and mine.

For the rest of my son's first day in the hospital, I reverted back to doing what I did as a patient—thinking. I was holding my child for the first time and all I could think about was the future.

Will I always be there for him? Will I live long enough with my health problems to see him grow up? Will I be able to go out in the yard and play catch with him like my Dad did? Will I be around to coach his Little League team?

All those thoughts were running through my mind. Scary thoughts. More to the point: negative thoughts.

I've since come to realize that dwelling on the future is only good in very small doses, if at all. No matter what the future brings, it's not going to change the fact that I have a child to provide for today.

Worrying about tomorrow doesn't help Cody. It only adds to

the anxiety of today and takes away from enjoying moments with him now.

One of the things I learned after facing all these challenges following my baseball career is that you can't go through life dreaming about yesterday or wondering about tomorrow. You've got to deal with today. Tomorrow can wait.

I spent the rest of 1994 enjoying quality time with Tricia and Cody, and re-establishing my insurance business with New York Life. In the previous two years, I had become more of a liability than an asset to the company because of my health problems. I couldn't meet my year-end quotas in '92 and '93, but the company was nice enough to give me a health-related waiver.

Well, I couldn't expect them to just keep giving me waivers. In our situation, we needed my job not only for income, but to maintain my health insurance. What employer is going to want to provide health insurance for someone with annual medical bills that run about $50,000?

That's not counting doctor visits or the transplant, which cost a quarter-million dollars. That $50,000 is just for my medication.

When I was sick, it was impossible for me to meet my year-end insurance quotas. Without New York Life and the patience it demonstrated, my situation would have been a lot tougher.

My first general manager, Chris Delahoussaye, and my current manager, Troy Braswell, really stuck by me through some difficult times. I wasn't producing much business for long periods of time and it would have been just as easy for them to say: "Sorry, Ed, we can't afford to keep you around."

In the beginning, it was probably a positive for the company to have a former pro athlete in the fold. But the bottom line is production and I wasn't producing. Still, I'll never forget the loyalty New York Life showed toward me when management could have justifiably taken the easy way out.

Ironically, nobody has a better built-in sales pitch to sell insurance than I do. As incredible as this might sound, I don't own a life insurance policy. I never bothered to buy one or even look into buying one until it was too late.

All those years I spent in professional baseball, it never dawned on me to do it. I was an athlete dealing with shoulder problems. Trying to get to the big leagues. Then trying to return to the big leagues.

I wasn't thinking about dying. Nobody ever does at that age.

Even though I had agents with backgrounds in accounting and investments, nobody ever mentioned life insurance. Tricia and I were married for almost four years when I was diagnosed with kidney failure and we never thought to buy a policy.

Now, of course, it's too late. When a childhood friend of mine learned about my medical condition and that I had no life insurance, he felt terrible because he was an insurance salesman. He never approached me about insurance because he figured I was already taken care of. He didn't want me to think he was trying to sell me something. What a mistake.

We can't buy that piece of mind now, but I urge you to learn from our misfortune—don't wait.

I almost wish I could relive 1995 all over again. It was probably the first year where I felt somewhat normal again and completely back in the real world.

The black and white was gone. I could really see the colors. For the first time in four years, I never had to stay in a hospital and I no longer needed psychiatric counseling for my depression. Physically, I had my ups and downs as far as energy level goes, but I felt much stronger mentally.

My speaking career had taken off way beyond expectations. People were calling me left and right to book engagements. I almost felt inadequate at times because of some of the large audiences put in front of me.

But there was no doubt about what was happening here—people wanted to hear my story because it uplifted them. The more I felt that positive energy, the more I began to feel that there was a real purpose to all the struggles I went through.

One really neat experience I had last year came at the Shell Houston Open golf tournament the last week of April. Tom, my younger brother, had earned his PGA Tour qualifying card, which earned us a unique place in history. We became the first brother combination to play Major League Baseball and on the PGA Tour. It had always been my hope to caddie for him when he got there.

Tom's pro career and mine had followed very similar paths. He played mini-tours for over seven years, battling through various injuries and the gamma globulin deficiency, before finally getting the opportunity to play his sport at the highest level. He even married a girl with the same first name: Tricia!

Now that he was on Tour, I just hoped I would be strong enough to carry his thirty-pound bag for four straight days.

Tom and I had a great time. I was tired at the end of each day, but the adrenaline rush of the competition kept me going. It was almost like I was part of a team again, even though all I did was make sure Tom's clubs were clean.

I didn't give Tom much input because he likes to do his own homework. He doesn't rely on a caddie as much as other golfers, but that was fine with me. I just wanted to get through each round without having to bail out on him.

The whole week was really a charge for me because for so many years, Tom had kind of lived in my shadow. It was nice to finally see him in the limelight, especially since he worked just as hard and faced many of the adversities I did trying to get to the top.

I remember when I was playing ball, Tom was probably as supportive of me as anyone. When things didn't go right for me back in my days with the Philadelphia Phillies organization, he was as angry as could be.

Now here my career was done and it was a great experience for me to share in Tom's success. There were times when I'm sure people felt he'd never make the PGA Tour. He ran into many bad breaks along the way, especially with the gamma globulin deficiency, but Tom gutted through situations where I'm sure many others would have given up.

In many ways, caddying for Tom was difficult because my emotions went up and down with him. One missed putt could make the difference between making the cut or going home after two rounds. It's tough watching a family member in that pressurized environment and it made me appreciate all the frustration my parents went through with me all those years.

Tom made the cut at the Houston Open and wound up winning $2,520. For my labor, I took home a grand total of $630 (the standard caddie fee of $500 plus five percent of Tom's earnings for the tournament). I later caddied for him at the Greater Milwaukee Open in August, but he missed the cut.

Unfortunately, Tom failed to finish in the top 125 on the money list, so he had to go back to Qualifying School. He didn't score well enough to regain his PGA Tour card, but will be competing on the Nike Tour in 1996.

Whether Tom makes it back up to the big leagues or not, I know it won't be for lack of perseverance. He took a hard road to get as far as he did in golf. One way or another, I believe his best payday is still ahead of him.

If there ever was any doubt about what I wanted to do with the rest of my life, it was removed a few days after I finished caddying for Tom in Houston.

I was booked for a speaking engagement in Dallas to talk to The Barons, which happens to be the top sales people for the western zone of New York Life. When they booked me through a speaker's bureau, they had no idea that I worked for New York Life.

It was a two-day conference and I shared the platform with three other speakers, including former Dallas Cowboys quarterback Roger Staubach and Les Brown, one of the top motivational speakers in the country.

At the end of my presentation, in which I relayed my own insurance horror story and my comeback from a kidney transplant, they gave me a standing ovation.

I also noticed when the audience was done clapping that I had an extra five minutes before they were due to take a break, so I went on to do something totally unplanned.

Usually, I go into every talk with a prepared game plan and stick to it. But I had this extra time and felt compelled to share something with the audience that I hoped would mean as much to them as it did to me.

Here's what happened.

The night before my talk in Dallas, something arrived in the mail at home that Tricia and I had anticipated for a long time, but weren't sure would ever come. An envelope contained two type-written letters, one from each parent of the eighteen-year-old boy whose kidney was now inside me.

These letters weren't mailed directly to us. The policy of the Organ Donor Bank is for the family of a deceased donor and the recipient to not know each other's identity. Any correspondence that either party sends must go through the donor bank. They screen letters and cards so there is nothing contained in them that would allow one party to identify the other.

I sent my first letter to my donor family back in October 1993. It was one of the hardest things I ever had to do. How do you properly thank the parents of a child whose organ is now in your body? What could I say that would provide any comfort?

In part, I wrote: *"I do not know if you have any desire to some day meet or even respond to this letter. I just want you to know my wife and I thank you from the bottom of our hearts for the miracle of life you have given to us. Thank you seems so trite, but they are the best two words I know.*

I must share with you that I believe everything that happens to us, happens for a purpose. And although your loved one is no longer with us in the flesh, I want you to know that he lives on... and together, we have touched many lives. May God bless you and keep you strong."

In December 1994, we also sent them our family Christmas card, which was partially censored to protect our identity. Inside that card was an organ donor card, encouraging our family and friends to sign up.

I can't begin to express the emotion I felt after Tricia faxed me those letters. At the speaker's podium in Dallas, it was all I could do to stay composed as I read excerpts from my donor parent's letter about their son, Chip.

Here's what Chip's father wrote: *"Personally, I was elated when your letter arrived. I was beginning to think that those who received Chip's kidneys and lungs gave little thought to the circumstances leading to that donation. Your letter proved me wrong. And your Christmas card touched me deeply."*

In the letter from Chip's mother, she wrote in detail about the circumstances that led to his fatal car accident, his dreams about wanting to be a policeman because he wanted to help people, and how that impacted their decision to allow his organs to be donated.

How difficult and courageous it must have been for her to write to us, saying: *"You wrote that you believe that everything that happens to us, happens for a purpose. I share that belief. I have spent many long hours searching for answers, and although I still don't know the specific reason for Chip having to leave us so early, I know that in the end, everything works for our own good. Some things are just beyond human comprehension.*

We would like you to know how very much we appreciate your statement that Chip lives on, that together you and Chip have touched many lives. It is very comforting for us to know that one of Chip's kidneys was given to someone who continually strives to make a difference in others' lives. It helps us believe that his early death was not entirely pointless."

Reading those letters in private was pretty emotional, but reciting those excerpts to a large audience was positively uplifting. When I was finished, the crowd gave me a second standing ovation. As I walked down the center aisle, Les Brown stepped out, grabbed me and gave me a bear hug, saying: "Man, that was awesome. What a great story and message."

Until that day, I had never met Les Brown. I only knew of his reputation as one of the best speakers in the business. It was really gratifying to hear that coming from him.

I hit a grand slam that afternoon in Dallas. From that

moment on, there was never a question in my mind that Ed Hearn was doing exactly what Ed Hearn was meant to be doing.

When I celebrated winning the World Series with teammates, then took part in a ticker-tape parade and went to the White House to hear President Reagan acknowledge us, I thought that was the ultimate. Nothing I'd ever do would surpass that for excitement or fulfillment.

But you never know what you're really capable of until situations or circumstances force you to strive beyond what you ever thought possible.

Even if I played in the big leagues another 10 years, maybe earned another World Series ring or two, I can honestly say I would not be impacting people's lives the way I do now.

I believe there's no greater satisfaction in life than knowing you've done something to help somebody else out. Whether that means going out and shoveling snow off someone's driveway or visiting them in the hospital, it doesn't matter. The size of the deed is irrelevant, but the satisfaction from serving someone in need is irreplaceable. That's something we all cherish.

I do treasure the time I spent in baseball. I still have many of my major league highlights at home on videotape. Occasionally, I'll pull them out to watch. But as nice as those memories are, they don't compare to the satisfaction I get from public speaking. I am paid to talk, but the greatest paychecks are emotional paychecks.

When people come up to you after a speech and say thanks for lifting them up, or express their gratitude for touching their lives in some way, you can't put a price on that.

On a few occasions, after talks I've given in the Kansas City area, people have said things like: "They may have called you the worst trade in Royals history, but after hearing you today, I think it was the best trade in Royals history."

I once thought there was nothing more important than becoming the next Johnny Bench. Life proved me wrong.

I once thought there was nothing sweeter than winning the World Series. Life proved me wrong.

I once thought all my medical problems and the adversities that accompanied them served no real purpose. Life proved me wrong.

Ten years ago, I was on top of the baseball world with the '86 Mets. Who knows if I'll even be here in another ten years?

But I know this: I'm alive, and I'm going to keep swinging for the fences, regardless of life's curves.

The Inside Pitch

It's Up to You

"Today is the tomorrow you thought about yesterday."

When we come face-to-face with our own mortality, often we begin to see life in a whole new perspective. We finally begin to realize the value of the little things. Unfortunately, it often takes some sort of crisis to shake us into reality.

Not long ago, I read a story that really illustrates this. It's about two men who were standing together in the older gentleman's bedroom. He opened a dresser drawer and took out one of his wife's slips. It was a gorgeous slip with an expensive price tag still hanging from the neckline. He said to his younger friend: "My wife bought this eight or nine years ago when we went to New York. It's a beautiful thing and she kept telling me she was going to save it to wear for a very special occasion." As he was standing there admiring it, he remarked: "You know, this must be that special occasion." And as he placed it on the bed along with some other things, he added: "I'm going to take this slip to the mortuary today."

We often go through life getting so caught up in this fast-paced world, we never take time to do those special things. We go trudging through our lives and it's always tomorrow we're going to do something.

Tomorrow we're going to do that favor for a neighbor. Tomorrow we're going to resolve a personal dispute by saying "I'm sorry." Tomorrow we're going to tell that special someone how much we love them.

But the next thing we know, our families are making funeral arrangements. Our life is over and we haven't even lived half of it.

In the final weeks before baseball great Mickey Mantle lost his battle with liver cancer, it was obvious the dramatic change that his illness had on him. Knowing his death might be imminent, The Mick expressed much heartfelt regret for so many things, from the alcohol abuse that contributed to his condition, to the way he neglected family relationships, to not being the proper role model that so many of his admirers wanted to believe he was.

Unfortunately, it took confronting his own mortality for The Mick to see the light. It took receiving a new liver from an organ donor on June 8, 1995, for him to right many wrongs in his last two months.

As sports announcer Bob Costas said in delivering The Mick's eulogy: "In the end, something remarkable happened, the way it does for champions. Mickey Mantle rallied. And what he did was stunning. The sheer grace of that ninth inning—the humility, the sense of humor, the total absence of self pity, the simple eloquence and honesty of his pleas to take heed of his mistakes."

To his credit, The Mick showed extraordinary courage when the end was near. By raising donor awareness to an all-time high, he may have done as much, if not more, in those final days for his fellow man than at any time in his Hall of Fame baseball career.

It's ironic that for his funeral, Mantle requested singer Roy Clark to play his favorite song, *Yesterday, When I Was Young*. It is a song that exemplifies why we should seize every moment, not live for time gone by or time we may never have.

The singer relays the story of his youth, of how he just ran with life, believing that he surely would have the time to sing all of those "happy songs waiting to be sung." But as he reaches the end of his life, he realizes with a great sorrow that he has wasted love and been overly concerned with himself instead of others.

There are so many songs in me that won't be sung,
I feel the bitter taste of tears upon my tongue.
The time has come for me to pay for yesterday,
when I was young.

243

I've played in Mantle's annual charity golf classic since my early days with the Kansas City Royals. At the 1994 tournament, he gladly consented to take a picture with our newborn son, Cody. When we returned last October, The Mick was gone. So was his chance to watch Cody dance with his two-year-old granddaughter, and so was our chance to witness first-hand The Mick's great, last-minute comeback.

On Mantle's promotional card for organ donation, printed after his death, he writes: "I'll never be able to make up all I owe God and the American people."

Oh, how The Mick's heart must have ached in his ninth inning. Not for his life being almost over, but for all that time lost. The time he could have spent doing things that he kept putting off until tomorrow. The time wasted that he spent wishing it was yesterday.

This lesson is summed up well in an old parable that says: "This is the beginning of a brand new day. God has given us this day to use as we desire. Now we can waste it or use it for good. But what we do today is important because we are exchanging this day of our lives for it. When tomorrow comes, this day will be gone forever, leaving in its place something we have traded it for. We want it to be gain, not loss. We want it to be good , not evil. We want it to be success, not failure, in order that we shall not regret the price we paid for it."

So I want to impress upon you the urgency of doing things NOW that enriches life. Some of us think we have a lot of time and one of these days we're going to get around to doing those things. Not just for others, but ourselves as well.

In laymen's terms, it's called procrastination. I call it the silent killer. It just kind of creeps along until pretty soon, it takes control of our lives. Then, before you know it, meaningless outside factors are keeping us from making a conscious effort to live life to the fullest.

As Amway founder Rich DeVos says: "The clock of time is wound and no one knows when the hand will stop, at late or early hour. Now is the time we have. Live, love and toil with a passion.

Place no faith in tomorrow, for the hands may then be still."
    If it's worth doing, do it now!

15

Epilogue

Donald L. Treese II
"Chip"
1973-1992

As the final chapter of this book was being sent to the publisher, a totally unexpected event took place. On January 18, 1996, Tricia and I received a phone call from our donor family. This came as a surprise to us because, although we expressed in letters a mutual desire to someday meet, the Organ Bank goes to a great deal of trouble to make certain that an organ recipient and the donor family will never know the other's identity.

Through clues that were left in our previous letters and a lot of diligent research, Donn and Kathy Treese of Pasadena, Maryland were able to locate me. When their phone call came, I was ecstatic. It was obviously an emotional occasion for all of us.

Even though we had corresponded by letters that were partially censored by the Organ Bank, an actual conversation is much different. There are so many feelings to express on both sides and greater apprehension because you don't know how much information the other party is willing to share. We certainly didn't want to say anything that might hurt or offend Chip's parents in any way.

Kathy made the initial call, which Tricia answered. She didn't want to speak to me at first because she wanted to find out from Tricia if I'd be receptive to talking, which I most certainly was. Since Donn was at work at the time, we agreed that we'd call them back later that night. The two-hour conversation that evening was one of the most uplifting moments for Tricia and me. Although I can't speak for Chip's parents, they seemed very happy and gratified that they initiated this get-together.

All Tricia and I knew about my donor was that he was an eighteen-year-old boy who had been killed in a car accident, that he served in the military and that he went by the nickname "Chip." His full name is Donald L. Treese II. I tried to identify my donor through some Army records, but I was never able to gather enough information to even get close. Chip's parents had a lot more clues about me and they put the final pieces together shortly after receiving my last letter on October 11, 1995.

It turns out that Chip, who was stationed at Fort Riley near Manhattan, Kansas—about 120 miles west of where we live outside Kansas City—passed away at St. Luke's Hospital. That's the same place where I had my kidney transplant. All Chip's parents knew about me initially was that I was a former major league ballplayer who lived in the Kansas City area. They were told that by a hospital employee shortly before leaving St. Luke's for the last time on the evening of April 26, 1992. Two hours later, I checked in to be tested to see if my donor kidney matched.

The first major clue for Chip's parents locating me came when we sent them our 1992 Christmas card. It contained a family picture on the front with a poem on the inside that Tricia composed about the happenings of that year. The Organ Bank blacked out the faces on our picture. But from scratching off the white-out on part of the poem, Chip's parents saw the name "Ed."

Knowing I was a former major league ballplayer, they started to research baseball almanacs at the library and going through baseball cards given to them by a co-worker of Chip's sister. My donor family narrowed it down to three possibilities.

In a follow-up letter that Chip's family received from me in

October 1995, I told them my height, weight, hair color, eye color, high school graduation year and that I sustained a career-ending injury. Matching that up with information on the back of baseball cards, they were able to uncover my identity.

But it still took them three months to contact us, partially out of apprehension and because they weren't sure whether to communicate by direct letter or phone.

In January, I called the Organ Bank to ask them if they could obtain my donor family's permission to use excerpts from their letters in this book. When Donn and Kathy learned that, they decided to make the call.

We're glad they did. Tricia and I have always wanted to express our appreciation in more than just letters. We've since had several heartwarming follow-up phone conversations. Perhaps very soon, we'll be able to meet our donor family in person.

But the main purpose of this epilogue is to remember Chip. He may be gone, but he's still here in many ways. Not only did I receive his gift of life, but so did three other people in various parts of the country. Another person received a kidney and two others his lungs.

Chip had served in the Army for eight months. He was on a weekend furlough at the time of the accident. Chip enjoyed playing soccer and writing short stories. He was the middle child of Donn and Kathy's three children. Ann is one year younger and Shannon is one year older.

More than anything, Chip wanted to become a policeman when he got out of the service because he wanted to help others. That selfless attitude is what convinced his family to give their consent for organ donation when the hospital staff brought it up. They had never discussed organ donation with Chip before.

Today, I'm still alive because of Chip's willingness to help out his fellow man. That's a testimony not only to his character, but to the way his parents raised him.

I'll never be able to do or say enough to repay the debt I owe Chip. I can only promise to live my life in an exemplary fashion that would properly honor his memory. **Thank you, Chip.** May

God bless your family and keep them strong.

WOULD YOU CONSIDER BEING AN ORGAN DONOR?

By completing the donor card below in the presence of your family and having them sign as witnesses, you'll know they pledge their support to see that your wishes are carried out. This donor card will serve as a reminder of your pledge to give the "Gift of Life."

ORGAN DONOR CARD

I, _____, have spoken to my family about organ and tissue donation. The following people have witnessed my commitment to be a donor.
I wish to donate the following:

☐ any needed organs and tissue.   ☐ only the following organs and tissue:

_____

Donor
Signature _____Date_____
Witness _____
Witness _____

Ed Hearn has become one of this country's most sought after motivational speakers. He speaks to groups ranging from youth groups and school districts to associations and corporations.

Gleaming from a lifetime of reaching for the top of life's mountain while experiencing the pits of its deepest valleys, Ed Hearn shares a wit and wisdom about life usually reserved for those much further along in years. Certainly his celebrity status of being a former major league ballplayer initially attracts many to ask him to speak, but be it young or old, executive or blue-collar worker, his audiences walk away remembering him not so much as an athlete, but more as a man who has had a dramatic effect on the way they view their own lives and challenges they face. They speak of being uplifted and inspired with a renewed spirit of hope and motivation to pursue victory in all areas of their lives no matter what the challenge or adversity. His courage, faith and motivation speak volumes to each of us as we face life's challenges in pursuit of the happiness and success we all desire.

*For more information about Ed Hearn's
inspiring motivational speaking,
call or write:*

*Triple Crown Success
9138 Allman
Lenexa, KS 66219
(913) 599-6586*

*Additional copies of Conquering Life's Curves
are available by calling:*

(913) 599-6586